KATY PERRY

Recent Titles in Greenwood Biographies

KATY PERRY

A Biography

Kimberly Dillon Summers

GREENWOOD BIOGRAPHIES

 GREENWOOD

AN IMPRINT OF ABC-CLIO, LLC
Santa Barbara, California • Denver, Colorado • Oxford, England

Library of Congress Cataloging-in-Publication Data

Summers, Kimberly Dillon.
  Katy Perry : a biography / Kimberly Dillon Summers.
    p. cm. — (Greenwood biographies)
  Includes bibliographical references and index.
  ISBN 978–1–4408–0100–6 (hardcopy : alk. paper) — ISBN 978–1–4408–0101–3 (ebook) 1. Perry, Katy. 2. Singers–United States–Biography. I. Title.
ML420.P4546S86   2012
782.42164092—dc23   2011053293
[B]

ISBN: 978–1–4408–0100–6
EISBN: 978–1–4408–0101–3

16 15 14 13 12   1 2 3 4 5

This book is also available on the World Wide Web as an eBook.
Visit www.abc-clio.com for details.

Greenwood
An Imprint of ABC-CLIO, LLC

ABC-CLIO, LLC
130 Cremona Drive, P.O. Box 1911
Santa Barbara, California 93116-1911

This book is printed on acid-free paper ∞

Manufactured in the United States of America

CONTENTS

SERIES FOREWORD

In response to school and library needs, ABC-CLIO publishes this distinguished series of full-length biographies specifically for student use. Prepared by field experts and professionals, these engaging biographies are tailored for students who need challenging yet accessible biographies. Ideal for school assignments and student research, the length, format, and subject areas are designed to meet educators' requirements and students' interests.

ABC-CLIO offers an extensive selection of biographies spanning all curriculum-related subject areas including social studies, the sciences, literature and the arts, history and politics, and popular culture, covering public figures and famous personalities from all time periods and backgrounds, both historic and contemporary, who have made an impact on American and/or world culture. The subjects of these biographies were chosen based on comprehensive feedback from librarians and educators. Consideration was given to both curriculum relevance and inherent interest. Readers will find a wide array of subject choices from fascinating entertainers like Miley Cyrus and Lady Gaga to inspiring leaders like John F. Kennedy and Nelson Mandela, from the greatest athletes of our time like Michael Jordan and Lance Armstrong to the most amazing success stories of our day like J.K. Rowling and Oprah.

While the emphasis is on fact, not glorification, the books are meant to be fun to read. Each volume provides in-depth information about the subject's life from birth through childhood, the teen years, and adulthood. A thorough account relates family background and education, traces personal and professional influences, and explores struggles, accomplishments, and contributions. A timeline highlights the most significant life events against an historical perspective. Bibliographies supplement the reference value of each volume.

OVERVIEW

Katy Perry was born Katheryn Hudson in Santa Barbara in 1984 to evangelical pastor parents, Keith and Mary Hudson. During her childhood, Katy took singing and dancing lessons. Her first singing performance was in front of a church congregation in the choir. She actually became interested in singing lessons because her older sister Angela was taking voice lessons and she wanted to do everything her big sister did. She used to sing her sister and her younger brother David to sleep at night, an activity that led to her nickname, "Katy Bird."

Katy had a sheltered childhood and moved around several times for her parents' ministry. The children were not allowed to listen to anything but Christian music. Katy's parents made sure that their friends only listened to Christian music as well. In the Hudson household, deviled eggs were angel eggs, *The Smurfs* could not be watched because of the sorcery and magic in the program, and they could not eat Lucky Charms cereal because the name was too close to that of Lucifer. Katy enjoyed herself by going to Christian camps and roller skating on Tuesdays, the rink's Christian night. Despite her parents' objectives, Katy's friends would sneak CDs to Katy so she could listen to pop culture musicians. She was greatly influenced by Alanis Morissette's album *Jagged Little Pill* and Freddie Mercury of the band Queen. It was at that time that Katy knew she wanted to be a pop star.

During her high school years, Katy sang in the choir and performed at the Santa Barbara Theater. One day during lunch she participated in an impromptu singing match where she was booed. While she was singing in her church, some Nashville producers heard her and liked what they heard. They encouraged Katy to follow her singing dream. Katy dropped out of high school to pursue her dream of being a pop star and received her GED in September 1999.

Katy and her mother went to Nashville to see producers in the gospel music industry, many of them acquaintances of the Hudson family. Katy signed with Red Hill Records and produced one album with them, *Katy Hudson*, with many of the songs written by her. The album was released but only about 200 copies were sold. The record label went bankrupt before it could market Katy's album. In search of a new record label, Katy signed with Island Def Jam, and when they let her go, she signed with Columbia Records. During this time she also changed her name from Katy Hudson to Katy Perry so she would not be confused with the popular actress Kate Hudson. She also wanted to distance herself from her first album that did not sell. While she was trying to make it as an artist, she took odd jobs to make ends meet, including a job at a music publisher. She had to sit in a cubicle and listen to other people's music and critique it. Katy realized that she could make it in the music industry because her music and style was different than anything she was hearing. One of the producers at Capitol Records, Chris Anokute, had heard Katy's music and thought she had a special talent. He tried to convince executive Jason Flom that Katy needed to be signed to the record label. After Anokute and Flom saw a performance in a nightclub, Flom was not impressed, but Anokute still assured Flom that Katy had an energetic, different style and would succeed. Flom eventually gave in and had a coffee meeting with Katy and signed her to Capitol Records. She has been soaring to the top ever since.

Katy Perry's first single, "Ur So Gay," from her album *One of the Boys* was released in November 2007. This brought little notoriety to Katy. The next single, "I Kissed a Girl," was the song that made people sit up and take notice. Although there was a lot of controversy over the lyrics, it soared to number one on the charts in the first week. The single sold 1.3 million downloads. The album sold 47,000 copies in the first week it was released. By the end of 2008, the album had reached platinum status with more than a million copies sold. With the success of the album came invitations and nominations for top award shows. She also set out on her first tour to promote herself, the *Hello Katy* tour. She also began to collaborate with other pop stars, such as Timbaland and Snoop Dogg.

Katy's second album, *Teenage Dream,* was much more than just an extension of the first album. It contained popular songs such as "California Gurls," "Waking Up in Vegas," and "Firework." In its first week, the *Teenage Dream* album sold more than 192,000 copies. By 2011, the album had reached platinum status. Katy tied with a record set by Michael Jackson: both had five number-one singles from the same album. Jackson's singles were from his album *Bad.* Katy's album *Teenage Dream* had the five singles, which were "Last Friday Night (T.G.I.F.)," "California Gurls," "Teenage Dream," "E.T.," and "Firework." With this latest release, Katy set off on her *California Dreams* tour, a tour that started in Portugal in February 2011 and ended in Dublin in November 2011.

The concerts were full of candy-covered sets and also used a technique called smell-o-vision. Katy made many costumes changes throughout the show. She did have to cancel two shows in Chicago and Minneapolis because she fell ill with food poisoning and severe dehydration. Katy's costumes were flamboyant and outlandish but they are what keep the fans interested. She has used whipped cream cans that actually squirted whipped cream in one of her acts.

Katy has not limited herself to the music scene. She has had guest spots and cameos on several television shows, including *Wildfire, The Young and the Restless,* and *How I Met Your Mother.* After her enormous musical success, she was invited on the popular talent shows *American Idol* and Britain's *The X Factor.* She was asked to appear on *The Simpsons* and *Sesame Street.* Her film credits include being Smurfette in the movie *The Smurfs,* which was released in the summer of 2011. This was an ironic part for Katy, since she was unable to watch the cartoon while she was growing up.

Katy's personal life has been in the press frequently as she has been busy making a name for herself in the music industry. In 2008 she dated Gym Class Heroes band member Travis McCoy. This was a short-lived relationship that ended in 2009. In September of 2009, Katy began dating actor Russell Brand. He had a checkered past of alcohol, drugs, and womanizing, but Katy looked beyond that and by the end of 2009 the two were engaged after a trip to India. Despite Brand's past, Katy's parents enjoy Brand and could not be happier for their daughter. In the media, however, the Hudsons claim they are always praying for the pair. Brand and Katy were married on October 23, 2010. Angela, Katy's sister, was the maid of honor. Katy flew her whole family to India for the private affair. Katy and Brand decided not to sell their wedding pictures to the media to keep their wedding day private and spiritual. Katy shared images from her October wedding at the Grammys. At the Grammy presentation, Katy descended onto the stage on a swing and was wearing a pale pink frock. While she sang "Not Like the Movies," the audience was treated to images of her wedding on a white backdrop. The first image was of Katy sharing a kiss with her new husband Brand. Once the slideshow was completed, she sang "Teenage Dream" while dancers did a musical number across the stage. Besides the big reveal of her never-before-seen wedding pictures, Katy heralded her *California Dreams* tour, which she was headed on after the Grammys.

As a celebrity, Katy has had her share of controversy. She has had disagreements with other musicians about her song lyrics, and things she has said have been misconstrued in the press. Her songs "I Kissed a Girl" and "Ur So Gay" created a backlash from church groups and the gay and lesbian community. Churches across the world believed the songs promoted homosexuality, and homosexuality is considered a sin and should not be condoned. The gay and lesbian community thought Katy was poking fun at their lifestyle. They also believed she did not know what she was talking about because she is not gay. Katy wrote and performed the songs because they were catchy tunes and dealt with something in her life experiences. Katy's style of dress has always been a topic of controversy, as many believe she dresses too provocatively. When she was invited on *Sesame Street* to do a skit about opposites with Elmo to the tune of her song "Hot N Cold," there was uproar that the wedding dress she was wearing was showing too much cleavage. After the video was leaked on YouTube, parents complained that the segment was too risqué for a children's show. The skit never aired on television.

Katy has used her talents to give back to the community as well. She supports HIV/AIDS research and breast cancer awareness. She has also contributed to relief in Japan and Australia with the purchase of wands from her tour shows. She has had a variety of charity giveaways on her Web site. She has participated in the program Tickets-for-Charity, in which a portion of all ticket sales goes to a charity of the buyer's choosing.

Katy has overcome many obstacles to be the pop star she is today. She has worked hard to be at the forefront of the music industry. She realizes her fans are her biggest asset in becoming a success. She continues to put energy into her albums and tours to keep her followers coming back.

ACKNOWLEDGMENTS

Many thanks to all those that patiently and enthusiastically support me through my writing endeavors. To my mother, Carol, and Steve, whose confidence in me has never waned; to my brother, Bill, who helped me editorially; my sister, Tracy, my cheerleader; my children, Lauren, Andrew, and Alex, and most of all my best friend, critic, and husband, John. Thanks to all the editors at ABC-CLIO who have helped me every step of the way. Thank you to George Butler at ABC-CLIO who has helped my writing career tremendously.

INTRODUCTION

Many young musicians struggle in the beginning to find the right genre and style that would eventually make them successful. Oftentimes it is a singer's background and experiences that craft their songs and who they are.

Katy was born to a pastor mother and a pastor father. She used her religious background to write about her faith. Many of Katy's first songs were asking questions about her faith. She went to Nashville to produce her first gospel album. Unfortunately, this was not the type of music that brought her the type of fame she was looking for. After several years of trying to sell her songs to different record labels, she changed her musical genre from Christian folk to pop music. She gave herself until the age of 25 to make it big or change careers.

Katy tried hard to break through the music industry with several music companies in the early 2000s, but without success. When she signed with Capitol Records, Katy had already been rejected by two other record labels. After taking odd jobs to make ends meet while using her free time to record demos, she finally found someone who recognized her talent and unique style. The executives at Capitol Records gave Katy the creative freedom to grow and to cultivate her own style. Their trust in Katy's talent proved fruitful when her first two songs reached number one on the Billboard charts soon after they were released. Her single debut, "Ur So Gay," proved racy and controversial and created a name for Katy Perry. Although she was already known to the public, she became an up and comer with her even more controversial hit, "I Kissed a Girl." Both of Katy's albums, *One of the Boys* and *Teenage Dream*, reached platinum status, with more than one million copies sold.

No one can become a celebrity without attracting controversy. Katy has an unconventional style of behavior and dress that has brought her to the forefront of celebrity buzz. Her explicit lyrics and racy album covers have sold millions of records and have placed her songs in the Top Ten Hits on the Billboard charts. Critics have claimed her lyrics are too racy, and some of her songs come with parental warnings. Others believe her choice of dress for her concerts and performances can be too flamboyant and revealing. With the advent of YouTube and iTunes, songs are also rated according to how many hits and downloads songs receive. Katy Perry's music has reached record numbers in both hits and downloads.

Katy does her best to keep her personal life out of the tabloids, but dating such celebrity bad boys as musician Travis McCoy and actor Russell Brand has made that difficult. Russell Brand and Katy's one-and-a-half year courtship was documented throughout the press. Their engagement in 2009 and their marriage in 2010 headlined celebrity magazines and Web sites. However, the Brands kept their wedding photos private, rejecting millions of dollars from the media, to keep them as mementos of their special day.

Before the age of 30, Katy had sold billions of albums and acted in several films and on television shows. To teenagers, her quick and controversial climb to the top is one of inspiration and hope that you can do anything that you set your mind to. Her individuality as a singer and a person is what people are drawn to. Fans keep coming back to her concerts because of the theatrical and fun things that happen. Having been compared to the likes of Madonna and Lady Gaga, in both dress style and music, Katy Perry has earned the right to fame and fortune.

TIMELINE: EVENTS IN THE LIFE OF KATY PERRY

October 25, 1984	Katheryn Elizabeth Hudson is born in Santa Barbara, California.
September 1999	Katy drops out of high school and receives her GED.
October 23, 2001	*Katy Hudson* album is released.
September 2004	Katy signs with record label Columbia Records.
October 2004	*Blender*, an American magazine, names Katy "The Next Big Thing."
March 10, 2008	Katy appears on an episode of the television show *Wildfire*, titled "Life's Too Short."
April 29, 2008	"I Kissed a Girl" debuts on iTunes.
May 6, 2008	"I Kissed a Girl" single is released; lyrics create much controversy.
May 21, 2008	The video of "I Kissed a Girl" premieres. It garners two million hits in two weeks.
June 12, 2008	Katy appears as herself on an episode of *The Young and the Restless*.

June 17, 2008   *One of the Boys* album is released in the United States.

June 17, 2008–
August 17, 2008   Katy joins *Vans Warped Tour* to promote herself and her recent album release, *One of the Boys*.

August 29, 2008   Katy performs her hit single "I Kissed a Girl" on the *Today Show*.

September 2008   More than 500,000 copies of the *One of the Boys* album are sold.

September 7, 2008   Performs at MTV Video Music Awards in Liverpool, England.

September 22, 2008   *One of the Boys* album is released overseas.

November 6, 2008   Hosts the MTV Europe Music Awards in Liverpool, England.

December 2008   Katy and Travis McCoy break up on a trip to Mexico.

January 23, 2009   *Hello Katy World Tour* begins in Seattle. Seventy-nine concerts are performed in the United States, Europe, Asia, and Australia.

January 27, 2009   *The Matrix* album is released in CD format and on iTunes. The album was produced in 2005.

February 2009   *One of the Boys* album goes platinum selling more than one million copies.

February 8, 2009   Katy performs "I Kissed a Girl" at the Grammys.

February 18, 2009   Attends Brit Awards in London. Receives International Female Award from Lionel Ritchie.

April 21, 2009   Katy's single "Waking Up in Vegas" is released.

May 13, 2009   Performs on *American Idol* singing "Waking Up in Vegas."

May 2009   Katy is seen with Travis McCoy at the Life Ball in Vienna, Austria. Rumors start that the two are back together.

June 9–10, 2009   Performs at O2 Shepherd's Bush Empire in London.

July 11, 2009   Plays Tin in the Park Festival in Scotland.

August 2009	Katy sits in as a guest judge on *American Idol*.
August 23, 2009	Katy performs at the Santa Barbara Bowl.
September 13, 2009	Katy meets Russell Brand at the MTV Video Music Awards at Radio City Music Hall in New York.
September 14, 2009	Katy goes on first date with Russell Brand. Gives Katy his autobiography *My Booky Wook: A Book of Sex, Drugs, and Stand-Up* and a black diamond necklace.
October 2009	Katy tweets that she enjoyed a week in Thailand. She had vacationed with Russell Brand.
November 2009	Both Katy and Russell take a trip to an Australian ski resort with the Hudson family.
November 5, 2009	Presents at MTV Europe Awards.
November 19, 2009	*MTV Unplugged* CD is released; Katy sings on the CD.
December 2009	Katy flies her entire family to New York for Christmas.
December 31, 2009	Katy and actor/comedian Russell Brand become engaged.
January 2010	Katy sits in as a guest judge on *American Idol*.
January 2010	Katy signs on as a Proactive skin-care advocate and does commercials for the product.
January 6, 2010	Publicists announce that Katy Perry and Russell Brand are engaged.
January 31, 2010	Katy attends Grammys, loses Best Female Pop Performance Award to Beyoncé.
March 27, 2010	Katy presents Favorite Movie Actress Award at Nickelodeon Kids' Choice Awards.
May 26, 2010	"California Gurls" single plays on radio. By the next day it is a number one hit.
June 2010	Katy is named #1 on *Maxim* magazine's "Hot 100" list. Katy is also named #37 in FHM's "100 Sexiest Women of 2010."
June 6, 2010	Katy attends MTV Movie Awards with Russell Brand.

August 2010	Katy is nominated for two Teen Choice Awards for "California Gurls."
August 24, 2010	*Teenage Dream* album is released.
September 12, 2010	Katy attends MTV Video Music Awards. She loses both her nominations to Lady Gaga.
September 14, 2010	Katy gives free concert to students at Dos Pueblos High School, where she went to school.
September 23, 2010	Statement is released that Katy Perry's skit with Elmo on *Sesame Street* will not air because of Katy's attire.
September 27, 2010	Appears on season opener of *Saturday Night Live*. Does a skit with an Elmo shirt that shows her cleavage in response to scratched Elmo skit on *Sesame Street*.
October 18, 2010	Katy performs her single "Firework" on the British talent show *The X Factor*.
October 23, 2010	Katy marries actor and comedian Russell Brand at the Aman-i-Khas Hotel in India.
October 26, 2010	Katy's hit "Firework" is released.
November 17, 2010	Performs "Firework" at MTV Europe Music Awards with a live fireworks display.
November 2010	*Cosmopolitan* magazine names Katy Perry Ultimate International Music Star.
November 11, 2010	Performs at Victoria's Secret Fashion Show in New York.
November 12, 2010	Katy's perfume Purr launches.
November 21, 2010	Performs at the American Movie Awards at Nokia Theater in Los Angeles, California.
December 2010	Katy participates in *USO Presents: VH1 Divas Salute to the Troops* to honor the military.
December 2010	Katy attends the Jingle Ball concert in a 3-D snowwoman dress.
December 5, 2010	Appears in *The Simpsons* episode "The Fight Before Christmas" as Moe's girlfriend.
January 2011	Katy's "Firework" is played during the Miss America Pageant.

February 13, 2011	Katy receives four Grammy nominations for Album of the Year, Best Female Pop Vocal Performance, Best Pop Collaboration, and Best Pop Vocal Album.
February 20, 2011	*California Dreams World* tour begins in Lisbon, Portugal.
April 21, 2011	Katy performs "E.T." on *American Idol.*
June 2011	Katy appears on the cover of *Vanity Fair* magazine.
July 20, 2011	MTV announces the nominations for the Video Music Awards. Katy receives nine nominations.
July 29, 2011	*The Smurfs* movie is released. Katy does the voiceover for the only female smurf, Smurfette.
December 2011	Katy and Brand announce they are seeking a divorce.

Chapter 1

"CALIFORNIA GURL"

Katheryn Elizabeth Hudson was born on October 25, 1984, in Santa Barbara, California. The child of born-again Pentecostal ministers, Katy enjoyed a happy, yet sheltered, childhood. Katy's older sister, Angela, was born in 1982 and her younger brother, David, was born in 1987.

Katy's upbringing was strongly influenced by her parents' desire not to expose their children to what they believed to be negative influences. Their own pasts helped form the decision to keep their children away from pop culture and other influences of society. Many believe that her restricted upbringing is the reason that Katy now has such an eclectic style of dress and why her lyrics are always controversial. Katy herself has said that she was looking for people's reactions early in life and was always looking for attention. "Her desire to perform, show off and basically draw attention to herself was thus established at an early age—something Katy has put down to 'middle child syndrome'."[1] In understanding Katy, it is important to know where she came from and her childhood background.

Keith Hudson was born in 1948 and was part of the "hippie" generation. Keith has four Jesus tattoos and has the look of a Harley rider,

typically wearing black T-shirts and jeans. He often has a large silver
cross dangling from his neck. He attended Woodstock and was said to
have hung out with Timothy Leary, the psychologist known for promoting the use of psychedelic drugs such as LSD, and during this time,
Keith took LSD. Musically inclined as well, Keith also played the tam-
bourine with the well-known band Sly and the Family Stone. During
this period, Keith also attended Christian revival meetings, where he
finally decided to change his ways and pursue a life of Christian ministry. It was at one of these tent revival meetings that he met Mary Perry.
Keith later said in his ministry that God spoke to him 39 years previously in an apple orchard in Washington. He said this calling transformed and saved him from the destructive life he was living with
drugs. Katy believed at that time that her father could speak in tongues,
which is described as a direct prayer to God. Katy said that while her
father spoke in tongues her mother translated what he was saying.

Mary Hudson came from a wealthy Santa Barbara, California, family. Her brother, Katy's uncle, was Hollywood producer Frank Perry,
who produced such films as *Mommie Dearest*, starring Joan Crawford.
Frank would often host parties at his Manhattan apartment, which
was Katy's first exposure to drag queens; she was fascinated with their
make-up and dresses. One of her favorite movies became *Paris Is
Burning*, a film about Harlem drag queens. Eleanor Perry, Katy's aunt,
was also in the movie industry. She was a screenwriter, who wrote the
comedy *Diary of a Mad Housewife*, a film for which Carrie Snodgrass
was nominated for an Oscar for Best Actress in a Leading Role. Of
German and Portuguese descent, Mary left her house at a young age
to become a hippie and a free spirit. She dated singer Jimi Hendrix
while she was traveling in Spain. Her travels took her to Zimbabwe,
where she married a race car driver who had lost his leg in a motorcycle
accident. The two moved to a nut farm in Zimbabwe and used his hol-
low leg to smuggle jewels for their antique business. After divorcing her
husband, Mary returned to the United States and became a reporter for
ABC Radio. She interviewed famous people, such as former president
Jimmy Carter and boxer Muhammad Ali.

Becoming born-again Christians saved Katy's parents' lives. They
traveled a lot during the first years with their ministry. During the
course of their traveling ministry, while Katy was growing up, the

Hudsons moved at least seven times. As it was a freelance ministry and their income was irregular, the Hudsons sometimes had to resort to food stamps to feed their three children. In Santa Barbara, the two founded the Christian Oasis Center. They now minister at a church north of San Diego called the Life Christian Church. During their services they often mention and pray for both Katy and her husband Russell Brand. While prophesying in London, Keith said to the congregation, "Anyone here heard of Russell Brand? He's my son-in-law. I love Russell. He's a wonderful man. We pray for him—pray for the entertainers."[2] They have welcomed Brand into their family with open arms. Keith attended the premiere of Brand's movie *Hop* with Brand. Katy's grandmother, Ann Hudson, attended the Grammys with Katy and Brand when she was 90 years old. All three of them, Brand, Katy, and Hudson, wore white Armani outfits and posed for pictures with the media. Katy had a bedazzled cane made for her grandmother for the event. To the amazement of the fans who were watching, Ann also commented on knowing Justin Bieber and Ryan Seacrest!

Keith and Mary continue to travel around America spreading the Word. Keith's ministry is called Keith Hudson Ministries, and it has its own Web site, www.keithhudson.org, and Facebook page. In 2009, Keith wrote a prayer book called *The Cry*. The book contains Bible passages and testimonials that come from the hearts of people who truly believe in the Word of God. Mary also wrote a book called *Smart Bombs*. In it she proclaims that the "word of God is similar to a modern-day smart bomb."[3]

Mary is also writing an autobiography, titled *Joyful Mother*. It is a book that relates how Katy has positively influenced her mother's ministry. Hudson insisted that the book she wrote about her family was not a tell-all about her daughter Katy but a book about her own Christian faith. Katy has stated in the media that her parents are supportive of her career and accept that she is different and does not practice or believe everything that they believe. She knows that her parents are happy and that they have three happy, successful children.

Mary views her and Katy's mother–daughter relationship as like other celebrity pairs that sometimes have a tumultuous relationship, such as Billy Ray Cyrus and Miley Cyrus, Britney Spears and Lynn Spears, and Jon Voigt and Angelina Jolie. Mary believes that her daughter has the gift of evangelizing, because despite the lyrics of her songs, which are not Christian, Katy has many followers because of her charisma and style. Like many other celebrity parents, Mary is afraid Katy is taken in by all the money, glitz, and fame that her success has given her. Mary does not agree with everything her daughter is doing, but is there to support her and help her in any way she can.

There were a number of things that Katy was not exposed to during her childhood, mainly dealing with pop culture. She was not allowed to read *Cosmopolitan* magazine because there was too much sex discussed in it and too much cleavage shown on the cover. In their household they did not talk about the pop stars of the time, such as Madonna, although Katy would later be compared to Madonna as a pop singer. Shows on channels such as MTV and VH1 were blocked from the Hudson television set. Because of the sorcery and magic associated with *The Smurfs*, that show was also banned in the Hudson household. The only music-related show Katy could watch as a child was the Grammy awards. The family did own a Nintendo, but were told to use the word "zap" instead of "kill." Deviled eggs were referred to as "angel eggs." There was no Lucky Charms cereal in the house because the name was too close to the name of Lucifer. The three children were not allowed to go to coed parties, not allowed to participate in sex education in school, and they were not allowed to view magazines, television, or movies where sex was a prominent theme. However, the three children would occasionally use the television passcode to watch certain shows when their parents were away. Katy went to a Planned Parenthood office to learn about birth control. She said, "I grew up in a sheltered household, and my parents would keep us from certain things they thought were too much for us and our eyes."[4] Katy's mom would only read the Bible to her children. Katy discovered the books about the young fictional character Eloise and was enthralled with them, because Eloise liked dresses and she lived in a hotel. Katy has said she feels she did not have a childhood and had to look for ways to entertain herself. She found an outlet in singing and performing when she was little.

Katy's first live musical performance was in the choir at church. She sang at the Oasis Christian Church until she was 16 years old. Katy did not aspire to be a pop star when she was growing up; she surrounded herself with kids who also listened to Christian music. In an interview with *Blender* magazine, Katy said, "[Non-religious] music wasn't allowed in the house because it's the Devil's work [according to her parents]. And if I brought home friends, my mom wanted to know if they were Christians."[5]

Her favorite Christian hymns in her childhood were "Oh Happy Day," "Amazing Grace," and "His Eye Is on the Sparrow." Katy's parents encouraged her to take singing lessons and she enthusiastically did so because her older sister Angela also took them. Katy always wanted to do things her older sister did. When Angela was not home, Katy borrowed her cassette tapes and practiced singing. After she had rehearsed the songs, Katy would put on performances for her parents. The associate pastor at their church, Manny Earnst, would call her "Katy Bird" because she was always singing in the choir. Her siblings also called her this fond nickname because she would sing them to sleep every night.

Although Katy had a strict upbringing, she did find ways to have fun. She went to religious summer camps and she would roller skate on Tuesday nights, because that was Christian night. She started skateboarding at the age of 13 and would go to Santa Barbara's East Beach to skateboard and to surf. She also loved having yard sales, an activity that she still enjoys to this day. She always visits thrift stores and flea markets in all the towns that she stops at while on her tours.

Katy went to church several times a week and would make an altar call to Jesus whenever she could. She also went to Christian schools and camps. When she was 13 years old she received a blue guitar as a birthday present from the church. This was when she started writing her own songs. She wrote her songs about faith and God, because that was all the music she had grown up with. She said, "All I really knew at that time was contemporary music, so I wanted to be like Amy Grant."[6] Many of the questions she had about her faith when she was a teenager were reflected in her early songs.

The Hudsons stopped traveling for their ministry and settled in Santa Barbara when Katy was 11 years old. At the age of 12 she auditioned at the Santa Barbara High School Theater for the production of *Fiddler on the Roof.* She attended Dos Pueblos High School in Goleta, California. During a lunchtime improvised singing competition, Katy was booed off the stage because she could not rhyme. Katy also joined the choir in high school.

It was also during her teen years that she became a tomboy and began to rebel a little bit. She started drinking and skipping school. It was when Katy had a Sunday morning hangover and she was crying that her parents divulged to her their own rebellious teenage years, to teach her a lesson. Her friends also began exposing Katy to pop-culture music during sleepovers. Her friends would sneak CDs for her to listen to in the privacy of her own room. Her favorite artists became Gwen Stefani, Alanis Morissette, and Freddie Mercury of the band Queen. She also enjoyed the album *Pet Sounds*, released in 1966 by The Beach Boys. Because of Katy's strict upbringing, she missed hearing music from artists such as New Kids on the Block, Madonna, and other '90s pop bands. The bands that are making a comeback and redoing their earlier hits are all new to Katy.

Katy's appearance also began to change when she started high school. She dyed her hair black. She believed she could show her individualism through her fashion choices—a belief that has held true throughout her music career. When she was a child she would dress up at least three times a day and wear different outfits at breakfast, lunch, and dinner. Katy was self-conscious about both her weight and the size of her cleavage. Since sixth grade she had been taping her chest so it didn't appear so big—a practice that she continued until she was 19 years old. While she was growing up, Katy wanted to look like model Kate Moss. Most of the time, Katy wore T-shirts and jeans or frumpy dresses. Many of her clothes came from thrift stores or vintage shops. Katy dropped out of high school to pursue her musical dreams and later received her GED in September of 1999.

During her childhood and teenage years, Katy always felt like the black sheep of the family. She constantly did things to get attention and felt the only attention she received was leftover attention. She has evidence of this attention-seeking behavior in the form of a scar on her ankle, the result of jumping off the roof at a pool party on a dare. She used her dark humor and sarcasm to get reactions from people. Katy's older sister, Angela, has said that the whole family is made up of attention seekers and is always looking to entertain people. Angela describes her childhood fondly, and has stated that she, Katy, and

David enjoyed fun and laughter. "We are like the Three Musketeers—actually the Three Stooges. I really feel blessed because of where I came from."[7]

Katy has carried religion into all aspects of her life. Her parents' ministry, although she does not agree with all its beliefs, has given her stability. In an interview with *Elle* magazine, Katy said, "I still do pray, though. I stay connected to religion that way, I guess, even though I don't agree with all the beliefs that I was brought up with."[8] While she was growing up, Katy even knew how to speak in tongues. After she met Russell Brand, she began to do Transcendental Meditation.

Despite her strict upbringing, Katy is thankful that her parents have been supportive of her career, although her father has talked to her about her provocative fashion style. She has no regrets about how her parents raised her. "She [Katy] has repeatedly said she has no regrets about her upbringing and is grateful to have a strong foundation to help guide her life."[9] After all, it was her mother who traveled to Nashville with Katy so she could make it in the music business.

NOTES

1. Dave Stone, *Russell Brand and Katy Perry: The Love Story* (London: John Blake Publishing, 2010), p. 40.

2. Roger Price, "Katy Perry's Parents Condemn Her Lifestyle While Cashing in on Her Eternal Damnation," *New York Post*, June 11, 2011. www.nypost.com

3. Jo Berry, *Katy Perry California Gurl* (London: Orion Publishing Group, 2011), p. 7.

4. Ruth Hilton, "Number One Crush." *Maxim*, January 2011, p. 56.

5. Stone, *Russell Brand and Katy Perry: The Love Story*, p. 40.

6. April Long, "Fantastic Voyage," *Elle*, March 2011, p. 399.

7. Rose Apodaca, "What Katy Perry Did Next," *Harper's Bazaar*, December 2010, p. 288.

8. Long, "Fantastic Voyage," p. 403.

9. Anne Brown, *Katy Perry*. People in the News Series (New York: Lucent Books, 2011), p. 76.

Chapter 2

"TEENAGE DREAM"

When Katy was 15 years old she attracted some Nashville producers when she was singing in church. Her family knew people in the gospel music industry in Nashville. She decided to take her chances and move to Nashville to produce a record. Her parents did not agree with the decision but Katy's mother traveled with her to Nashville. According to Katy, "We [she and her parents] agreed to disagree and move on."[1]

Katy started playing the guitar and writing her own songs when she was 13 years old, so she already had a repertoire of songs. In the early days when she was recording her gospel songs and the album, Katy superglued the tips of her fingers because they hurt from playing the guitar all day long. One of her first songs was titled, "Trust in Me." When she got to Nashville she signed with the Christian music label Red Hill under the direction of Jennifer Knapp and Steve Thomas. Her first album was categorized as a Christian gospel album and was called *Katy Hudson*. Katy wrote four of the songs herself and co-wrote the other six songs. Katy spoke about the songs on the album and specifically about the song "Trust in Me." She said, "It ("Trust in Me") ended up going on the gospel album I recorded when I was 15. All the songs I wrote (at that time) were related to my faith and the questions I sometimes had about it."[2] The album was a Christian pop-rock album and was greatly influenced by Alanis Morissette. Although the album received good reviews by the critics, *Katy Hudson* sold only about 200 copies. There was no money or budget at Red Hill to promote the album properly. Red Hill eventually went bankrupt and the *Katy Hudson* album became obsolete and hard to find. Because of Katy's popularity now, a fan may be able to find a vintage copy of the album on the Internet for $75–$100.

By the age of 17, Katy had already produced an album and had been dropped by a record label. She continued to make demo recordings and meet with producers to further her career. She came to realize that she needed to work hard and make sacrifices in order to make it big in the music industry. After being rejected by the music label, Katy did not get discouraged. She took a class on how to write songs and had people teach her how to play the piano and the guitar. In an interview with *Us Weekly*, she said she realized, "Putting out a record doesn't mean you're famous."[3] She did everything she could to get her name and sound out in the public. She sang in nightclubs and her manager at the time, Clifford Scamara, encouraged her to do Christian performances at various fairs and festivals.

Katy saw producer Glen Ballard on a VH1 show talking about Alanis Morissette and her successful album *Jagged Little Pill*. Ballard won three Grammy awards for *Jagged Little Pill*. He began writing songs in 1975 for Kiki Dee. He also wrote songs for George Benson, the Pointer Sisters, and Patti Austin. He also worked with Annie Lennox, No Doubt, and Dave Matthews. He co-wrote Michael Jackson's hit "Man in the Mirror" and Christina Aguilera's song "The Voice Within." His credits also include writing "Pink" by Aerosmith and "I Wonder Why" for Curtis Stiger. Katy wanted an interview with Ballard. After her CD didn't sell, she got an audition with Ballard. Recognizing Katy's talent, Ballard encouraged Katy to return to Los Angeles and continue writing songs, and he signed Katy to his label.

Upon her return to Los Angeles, Katy gave herself a deadline. She had until the age of 25 to have a successful music career or she would give up. She changed her hair from sandy blonde to brunette. She also changed her name from Katy Hudson to Katy Perry so she would not be confused with popular actress Kate Hudson. She also wanted to distance herself and her name from her unsuccessful Christian album. Katy sang backup vocals and wrote songs for other singers. She sold her clothes to vintage stores and asked her parents for money to survive. During this lean stage in her career, she had two cars repossessed and she was writing bad checks, but she was determined to have her musical dream come true. Katy also began drinking during this time when she could not find work. She was desperately trying to get her career off the ground, but also was having fun partying at night. It came to a point that Katy realized that she would have to stop drinking to excess and concentrate on her music and songs 100 percent if she wanted to succeed.

By the age of 19, Katy had signed her second record deal, with Island Def Jam. The label planned a release date of 2005 for her album. It was in 2004 that she was working on her own solo album and with the band, The Matrix. The band had also worked with music stars Avril Lavigne and Shakira. The group was composed of Lauren Christy, Graham Edwards, Scott Spock, and British singer Adam Longlands. They had invited Katy to be a vocalist on their first album. The single, "Broken," by The Matrix featured both Katy and Longlands in the video. The band did not release the album in 2004, so it was another disappointment in Katy's beginning music career. The album was finally released in 2009 on The Matrix's own record label, Let's Hear It Records.

Island Def Jam decided not to release Katy's solo album and dropped Katy from the record label. Some of her songs, however, did make it into the public forum. She used her songs "Box," "Long Shot," and "Diamonds" on both YouTube and her MySpace page. Her song, "Simple," was on the soundtrack of the film *Sisterhood of the Traveling Pants*. Katy was given a reason for her dismissal from Island Def Jam. "The explanation was that they simply did not know how to market Perry's music and her style."[4] Even though the album was not released, Katy was tagged by *Blender* magazine in September 2004 as "The Next Big Thing." She also was mentioned in *Teen People* as "The One to Watch."

Shortly after being let go by Island Def Jam, Katy signed with Columbia Records. Columbia Records would not let Katy be creative in her style and lyrics, according to her manager Brad Cobb. Publicity executive for Columbia Records, Angelica Cob-Baehler, was talking with Chris Anokute at the Grammys. Anokute was an executive in charge of looking for fresh talent at Capitol Records. Cob-Baehler took the opportunity at this encounter to tell Anokute that Columbia Records was going to let Katy go. In a matter of several weeks, Columbia Records had let One Republic, The Jonas Brothers, and Katy Perry go. Katy wrote two songs on Kelly Clarkson's *All I Ever Wanted* album, "I Don't Hook Up" and "Long Shot." Katy wrote "I Don't Hook Up" with Greg Wells and Kara DioGuardi, who is now a judge on the U.S. talent show *American Idol*. "Long Shot" was written with Katy's producer Glen Ballard and Matt Thiessen, who is the lead singer of the band Relient-K. Since there were only 12 tracks on her *One of the Boys* album, "Long Shot" and "I Don't Hook Up" did not make the cut. Clarkson heard the songs and liked their unique sound. "I Don't Hook Up" was a Top 40 hit for Clarkson. Again, being let go by a record label left Katy searching for someone who believed in her and her music.

During this time Katy did everything to stay within the music industry while trying to make ends meet. She was in several music videos for different bands. She did background vocals for the band P.O.D. (Payable on Death), a Christian metal band, for their single "Goodbye for Now," on their album *Testify*. She also appeared in the music video for the song "Goodbye for Now." She was in the music video "Learn to Fly," by the group Carbon Leaf. With Gym Class Heroes, she appeared in the music video for "Cupid's Chokehold," as the love interest of band member Travis McCoy, a role she would play in real life. On 3OH!3's album *Want*, she sang with the band on their single "Starstrukk." After being rejected so many times by music labels, Katy began writing with musician and producer Dave Stewart, who is known for his work with the band Eurythmics. During this transition period, Katy also took a job with Taxi Music, a music publisher. Her job was to sit in a cubicle and listen to other people's songs and find new talent. She realized in doing that job that there was no one in the music industry that had the same vocal style that she did. This feeling helped her overcome the rejection of being let go from several music labels. It made Katy more determined to find someone who would listen to her demos and her unique sound. "I saw other girls come and go. I wondered if there would

Katy takes part in the "Red Is for Emmy" campaign in Los Angeles to benefit children. (AP Photo/Branimir Kvartuc.)

still be space for me. But I knew I was different. I'm a big goofball who speaks her mind, and there's always room in music for someone with a strong vision."[5]

That vision and special talent would be seen by Chris Anokute at Capitol Records. At the Grammys, when Cob-Baehler told Anokute that Katy was being let go, she also gave him a demo copy of Katy's song "Waking Up in Vegas." Anokute believed that the song was vibrant and Katy could be a bright new star. He brought the track to his boss Jason Flom. After hearing it, Flom was not as impressed with the song as Anokute. Anokute and Flom went to one of Katy's performances at the Viper Room on the Sunset Strip. Neither was overly impressed with Katy's performance. Despite the disappointing set, Anokute still believed that Katy possessed something unique and different than other musicians. Cob-Baehler eventually also moved as an executive from Columbia Records to Capitol Records. Both Anokute and Cob-Baehler were then pressing for Flom to make a deal with Katy and sign her to the label. Flom soon gave in and set up a coffee meeting with Katy. It was at this meeting that Katy signed to her fourth record label Capitol Records and was on her way to an extremely successful and record-breaking career.

NOTES

1. April Long, "Fantastic Voyage," *Elle*, March 2011, p. 399.

2. Jo Berry, *Katy Perry California Gurl* (London: Orion Publishing Group, 2011), p. 8.

3. Michael Steele and Editors, *All About Katy Perry, Us Weekly Special Edition*, September 2011, p. 33.

4. Anne Brown, *Katy Perry*, People in the News Series (New York: Lucent Books, 2011), p. 27.

5. Jo Berry, *Katy Perry California Gurl*, p. 32.

Chapter 3

COMING TO LIFE

By the end of 2007, Katy was doing well in her professional career. She had signed with music conglomerate Capitol Records. They immediately looked for ways to expose Katy's musical talents to the public. Katy took the signing with Capitol Records with dignity and did not let the signing go to her head. She knew she still had a lot to prove as a musician. She realized that nothing was going to be given to her without her own hard work and determination. She creates songs that play to people's emotions and make them think about their lives. Katy's songs are multi-generational. Both parents and teenagers enjoy Katy's catchy tunes. Katy creates events for her songs. Each song becomes a mini-movie or Broadway show that is carried through the video and on her concert tours.

Katy began working with Lukasz Gottwald, known as Dr. Luke, producing and writing songs. Dr. Luke had also worked with such stars as Britney Spears, Kelly Clarkson, Avril Lavigne, and Miley Cyrus. Katy worked with other writers and producers in the studio. She even worked at home writing songs after spending all day in the studio. What came of those sessions were two songs, "Hot N Cold" and "I Kissed a Girl." She worked on the songs "Ur So Gay" and

"Mannequin" with Greg Wells. They first introduced Katy to the public with the video version of "Ur So Gay." The video was directed by Walter May. The single was slapped with a Parental Advisory sticker in the United States.

Katy went on the Vans Warped Tour in 2008 to promote herself. The Warped Tour began in 1994 to promote new pop bands and musical acts. The band or performer plays for 35 minutes and could be on any one of 10 stages. The concert goes from 11 am to 9 pm. Since 1994 it has become a large festival where fans can hear some of their favorite artists and get band merchandise. The tour sometimes has more than 100 participants and tours throughout the United States and Canada. On the 2008 tour that Katy participated in, the bands included Reel Big Fish, Angels and Airwaves, and Gym Class Heroes. Overall Katy's experience with the Warped Tour was a positive one. She worked hard throughout the day, sometimes in grueling hot conditions. In Cincinnati, Katy was met with some not-so-nice fans. The audience threw things on the stage while she was performing. While at the Riverbend Amphitheater, the crowd seemed bored with Katy's performance, even though she sang her controversial hits "I Kissed a Girl" and "Ur So Gay." This reaction did not deter Katy from finishing her set, despite the crowd trying to hurry her along. One explanation of the Cincinnati crowd reaction by some critics was that the Warped Tour does not have many pop-oriented musicians and the fans may just not have been interested in Katy's type of music.

The first album Katy did for Capitol Records had six songs that were on the Def Jam album that were never produced. She did a video for one of those songs, "Ur So Gay." The single of the song was released in November 2007, but only a few thousand copies were sold.

It was with the release of Katy's second single, "I Kissed a Girl," that people started to take notice, mainly because the lyrics were so controversial. Katy wrote the song with British singer Cathy Dennis. Dennis had also helped other musicians, including Kylie Minogue with her song "Can't Get You Out of My Head" and Britney Spears with the song "Toxic." Dennis Reese, the SVP of Promotions at Capitol Records, also saw the talent that Katy possessed and agreed with Anokute that her songs needed to be exposed on a larger level. Reese pushed the song to be released on national radio to get the most

On June 9, 2008, Katy appears at MTV's Total Request Live show in New York. (AP Photo/ Evan Agostini.)

exposure as possible. The single debuted on iTunes on April 29, 2008. The music video was released on May 21, 2008, on MySpace. By June 3, 2008, the single had reached number one on the iTunes Top 100. On May 6, 2008, "I Kissed a Girl" was first heard by the public via a media outlet, on the Nashville radio station The River.

The "I Kissed a Girl" video was released in 2008 on Katy's Web site. The video featured Katy and other exotically dressed women dancing to the song. The video does not exhibit any same-sex kissing as implied by the title. The video was directed by Kinga Burza. The video premiered on television in the summer of 2008 on TRL. It placed number 20 on VH1's Top 20 Video Countdown in June and by July had soared to number four on the VH1 Countdown. More than 30 million views of the video had been logged on YouTube. By 2011, a disclaimer had been placed on the video on YouTube and viewers had to be 18 or older to view "I Kissed a Girl."

Shortly after, on June 17, 2008, Katy's first album under Capitol Records, *One of the Boys*, was released. In its first week out, the album sold 47,000 copies. With the recent advances in technology, a song's success is also measured in downloads to iPods and other MP3 players. "I Kissed a Girl" sold 3.1 million downloads. It was ranked by *Billboard* magazine as the ninth-highest-selling album in the United States and stayed on the *Billboard* "Hot 100" for seven weeks. "I Kissed a Girl" reached another Billboard record by becoming the thousandth Billboard number one hit of the rock era. Katy beat out band Coldplay for the honor. It was also the first time in 41 years that two artists from Capitol Records held the top posts in the charts. Coldplay's hit "Viva la Vida" was the song that led the band to history-making records. The song was also used in the teen drama series *Gossip Girl*. By September 2008, the *One of the Boys* album had sold a staggering 500,000 copies. Musicians equate their first album success by record sales and music critic reviews. Obviously sales of the album were reaching the numbers that Capitol Records was hoping for. Anokute was proven correct about Katy's talent and uniqueness of her style with her first album. The reviews for Katy's first album were mixed. Some enjoyed the creativity but others thought the songs lacked meaning and focus. Katy writes many of her songs from real-life experiences and all the emotion in the songs comes from her heart. In an interview with *Seventeen Magazine*, Katy said, "I really enjoy that music has such an effect on people—whether you're feeling happy, or you're crying as you're driving down the road. I love that a song can trigger a moment."[1]

Critics had dubbed Katy's *One of the Boys* album as a pop album. They claimed the only topic covered on the album was love. They believed "Waking Up in Vegas" was a catchy tune that people would not be able to sing along with and commented that "Thinking of You" was a well-written ballad. Critics believed the album began with strong tracks and ended with songs people would not listen to. Others could tell that Katy had a lot of fun recording this album because they could hear it in her songs. It was hailed as one of the best albums of the summer.

By the end of 2008 the *One of the Boys* album had reached platinum status with more than one million records sold. The album also produced three Top 10 singles, including "Peacock," "Circle the Drain," and "Hot N Cold." Katy also went on a tour of radio stations to promote the album. Success for the album also meant success for Katy as a musician and celebrity. She was nominated for Best Female Artist at the 2008 MTV Video Music Awards in Los Angeles. Her video was also nominated for Best Female Video, Best Art Direction, Best Editing, and Best Cinematography at the MTV Video Music Awards. She lost Best Female Video to Britney Spears and lost the Best New Artist nomination to Tokyo Hotel for the song "Ready Set Go." At the 2008 Video Music Awards, Katy sang Madonna's hit "Like a Virgin" with Travis Barker and DJ AM. DJ AM was found dead in his apartment in August 2009. Katy took to Twitter and offered her condolences to his family and friends. She also praised him and said what a talented artist he was. She was invited to co-host the MTV European Music Awards held at the Echo Arena in Liverpool, England. During the awards, she won the Best New Act Award. She was also nominated for the Most Addictive Track with "I Kissed a Girl" but lost to Pink for her song "So What."

On January 23, 2009, Katy set off on her first world tour to promote the *One of the Boys* album. She called it the *Hello Katy* tour. She played to sold-out crowds all over the world. It was supposed to be a one-year tour that took her to Asia, Europe, Australia, and the United States. In February she took a break from the tour to perform at the Grammys. She sang her single "I Kissed a Girl." At the Grammys she also flaunted her fruit-themed attire. She came on the stage on a vertical banana and had the stage covered in fruit. Shortly after, on February 18, 2009, Katy attended the BRIT Awards in London. She was nominated and won the Best International Female Solo Artist award. She accepted the award from fellow singer Lionel Ritchie. Unfortunately, Katy had the flu at the awards but was told her attendance would be rewarded so she showed up. Her acceptance speech made mention of her being under the weather. She said, "I just want to thank everybody here in London and in the UK. I am so sick right now but they said I should show up to the BRITs because something special might happen, so thank you very much."[2]

In 2009, Katy went on the road to promote herself. She spent much of 2009 traveling and developing a fan base. On June 9–10, 2009, she played at the O2 Shepherd's Bush Empire in London and in July, she was in Scotland playing at the Tin in the Park Festival. During

the festival, many of Katy's adorning male fans held up marriage proposals for her. She did address the proposals during her concert, saying
that her answer to all of them was no. Other fans gave their phone
numbers, requesting calls from Katy. To stick with the candy/fruit
theme of her videos and concerts, she threw inflatable strawberries into
the crowd. She ended the festival with one of Queen's hits, "Don't Stop
Me Now," and her controversial hit "I Kissed a Girl." In August she
performed at the V Festival in Essex Weston Park in Staffordshire. By
the end of August, in 2009, she was back in the United States at the
Santa Barbara Bowl. She was present on the awards circuit as well. In
September 2009, she attended the MTV Music Awards in New York.
She opened the show singing Queen's "We Will Rock You" with Joe
Perry on the guitar. Katy was nominated for Best Female Video for
the song "Hot N Cold." She was a presenter at the MTV Europe
Awards in Berlin in November.

Katy was asked by MTV to appear in their promotional skit to
advertise the Video Music Awards. The promotional skit was a *West
Side Story* theme and included celebrities Taylor Swift and Russell
Brand. Katy received the part of Anita but thought she should have
played Maria, the part that Natalie Wood played in the movie, because
she has brown eyes and brown hair. In an interview with *MTV News*,
Katy explained, "I play Anita. Although I know I should be playing
Natalie Wood, because I've got the big eyes and the brown hair. But
everyone keeps telling me Anita is hotter, cooler, and sluttier. So
I can relate to that!"[3] Katy looked forward to participating in the
Video Music Awards. She had to outdo herself from last year's costume,
when she appeared in a jumper with a big banana on it. Costume
changes have become a tradition with Katy in both her concerts and
in her award show presentations. She had become a successful singer
as her album, *One of the Boys*, garnered many top singles on the charts.
She was nominated for Best Female Video for the hit "Hot N Cold."
The other nominees in the Best Female Video category were
Beyoncé's "Single Ladies (Put a Ring on It)," Kelly Clarkson's "My
Life Would Suck Without You," Lady Gaga's "Poker Face," Pink's "So
What," and Taylor Swift's "You Belong With Me." Swift took home
the Best Female Video Award.

In 2009, Katy was also collaborating with other musicians. She sang with Timbaland on his *Shock Value II* album. The two sang "If We Ever Meet Again," which was a different style for Timbaland because it was a song, not a rap. The song is about meeting someone special, and Timbaland believed Katy was the perfect person to sing about that. Timbaland's hopes for the song were that he wanted to have depth and be serious. Katy appeared in the video in a skimpy black dress with black boots, playing an alleged burglar. Critics criticized the song and video as not being one of either Timbaland's or Katy's best work.

The following year, 2010, proved lucrative for Katy in the awards department, as well as financially. At the 52nd Grammy Awards, Katy was nominated for Best Female Pop Performance for "Hot N Cold." She attended the Nickelodeon's Kids' Choice Awards on March 27, 2010, at the University of California, Los Angeles. Her song "I Kissed a Girl" was nominated for Favorite Song at the awards. In June, Katy attended the MTV Movie Awards with her fiancé Russell Brand. At the awards, she and Snoop Dogg sang their collaboration, "California Gurls." Katy made an appearance at the MTV Video Music Awards in September, where she was nominated for Best Female Video and Best Pop Video but lost both nominations to Lady Gaga for her song "Romance." In November 2010, Katy performed "Firework" at the MTV Europe Music Awards in Madrid. She won the Best Video Award for "California Gurls." "California Gurls" was also dubbed as the Song of the Summer for 2010, according to VH1.

In November 2010, Katy performed a concert at the Roseland Ballroom in New York to promote Windows-based products, especially the new Windows-based phone that was released. Katy began the concert by jumping out of a cake. During the performance, she mentioned the Windows software company several times. The repertoire of songs included "Hot N Cold," "I Kissed a Girl," "Ur So Gay," "Peacock," and "Teenage Dream." She kept her song "California Gurls" for the last song of the evening. She also threw out beach balls to the audience during the last song, to interact with the crowd.

Katy used her personality and celebrity to perform a concert in Times Square at the Crossroads of the World Stage to introduce the new 2011 Volkswagen Jetta. Katy sang "I Kissed a Girl," "Hot N

Cold," and "California Gurls." Her costume was true to her outlandish personality and was a neon green, skintight dress complete with palm trees. She ended the concert by doing a sing-along with the crowd while dancing on the hood of one of the demonstration Volkswagens.

The culmination of 2010 for Katy was her nomination for four Grammy Awards. She received a nod for Album of the Year for *Teenage Dream*, Best Female Vocal Performance for "Teenage Dream," Best Pop Collaboration for "California Gurls" with Snoop Dogg, and Best Pop Vocal Album for *Teenage Dream*. Unfortunately, Katy did not win any Grammy Awards. She lost Album of the Year to Lady Antebellum's *Need You Now*; Best Female Pop Vocal Performance went to Lady Gaga for "Romance." She and Snoop Dogg lost the Best Pop Collaboration Award to the song "Imagine," performed for The Imagine Project by Herbie Hancock, Pink, India, Arie, Seal, Konono N° 1, Jeff Beck, and Oumou Sangare. The Best Pop Vocal Album went to Lady Gaga's album, *The Fame Monster*.

While she was making appearances everywhere in 2010, Katy was also in the studio working on her second album. The fan base that Katy was trying to reach with her songs is the teenager who is looking for true love and all the obstacles that are encountered along the way. The challenge for a musician in making his or her second album is first, to have it be better than the previous album and second, to create new and refreshing songs that fans will enjoy and sing along with. An artist's second album is often referred to as their sophomore album. Many musicians disappoint their fans by putting out a sensational first album and then falling into the "sophomore slump" for the second album. This was not the case with Katy's *Teenage Dream* album. Katy had her own thoughts about what she wanted the album to sound like after being on tour for almost a year. Katy learned during her concerts and performances the emotions that she wanted to evoke with her fans. For her second album, her objective was to have fun and to produce songs that would make people dance around to her quirky songs. "When I was touring I wanted people to dance more. So I wrote an album that made people move, yet didn't sacrifice the story substance that I had on the last album."[4] Elliot Wilson of RapRadar.com enjoyed Katy's naiveté on her second album and the fact that she doesn't try to be perfect like other musicians, she just wants to have fun. In an interview with MTV *News,* Wilson commented, "She has a rock-chick kind of attitude, but at the same time she can pass for a pop princess. What I like about Katy Perry is that she seems kind of rebellious. People want to peg what the artists should be, and then you see the artist's growth, and I think that she's challenging. I think she's brash and bold."[5] Other critics have also praised Katy for working hard to make her songs fun and appealing for fans.

Capitol Records gave Katy the go-ahead to be more creative on her second album. They brought on new artists and producers to make a different, more mature-sounding album. The album took only six months to create but it was rewritten four times. The album was written with Bonnie McKee, Thaddis Kuk Harrell, Rivers Cuomo, and Ryan Tedder. Rivers Cuomo is the frontman for the band Weezer. In 2009, he and Katy had collaborated on a few songs for her second album *Teenage Dream.* Katy wanted a new sound for her second album so it didn't appear to be just an extension of her first album, *One of the Boys.* She used Cuomo to help her achieve a new and different sound while not alienating her fans, who took so well to her first album and its singles. Tedder is the leading man for the band OneRepublic and writes songs for artists in his free time. He created many catchy tunes for Katy. Because of their busy schedules, Katy and Tedder were hard-pressed to get together to create the songs.

The songs on the album were written out of Katy's own experiences. "California Gurls" was written about California after Katy listened to the Jay-Z and Alicia Keys song "Empire State of Mind." Katy believed "California Gurls" needed to be written because guys dream about California girls. In the song, Katy revealed that there are many assets, aside from girls, in California. The state also has palm trees, sun all the time, and sun-kissed faces, according to the lyrics. Katy's song was also the only California song that was written from a female perspective. She recorded the song with Snoop Dogg. Originally the song was titled "California Girls" but was changed to "Gurls" in remembrance of Alex Chilton. Katy's manager suggested the change because of Chilton's song "September Gurls," recorded in 1957. Chilton died of a heart attack on March 17, 2010. "California Gurls" became number one on iTunes almost immediately after it was released. Within four weeks, more than a million downloads were sold. By the end of the month, the song had made it to the top of *Billboard* magazine's "Hot 100" chart. The video, set in Candyfornia, had more than six million hits within the first week of being on YouTube.

Cebu Pacific Airlines, based out of the Philippines, also used the song during their in-flight safety presentation. The safety demonstration also included Lady Gaga's song "Just Dance." The airline company used the two popular hits because it has always been described as a fun airline. Executives wanted to bring fun into a boring safety demonstration and bring it alive. The basic demonstration was shown to passengers while they were still grounded but then when the plane was in the sky, flight attendants were dancing and demonstrating in the aisles.

Katy's "I Kissed a Girl" song was inspired by Scarlett Johansson. Katy has said in the press that she finds Johansson interesting and she is an attractive lady. The song "Not Like the Movies" was inspired by Russell Brand and is a song about falling in love. Katy believes that falling in love should be like it is in the movies and if not, you may be selling yourself short and perhaps you should wait until it does.

"Firework" has inspired many fans to be what they want to be and achieve greatness. Many organizations have used this song to inspire volunteerism and patriotism. Katy wrote this song with the belief that everyone possesses a special spark within them; they just have to find it and cultivate it. In the video for the song, Katy shoots sparks from her chest. There are many activities in the video that suggest that Katy's intention for the video was to be who you are and show everyone your spark. The video was dedicated to the It Gets Better Project. The project sends the message to gay youth that there is hope despite all the bullying and teasing that they may have to endure for their lifestyle. The song "Firework" became one of the most inspirational songs of the year. In January the song was played at the Miss America Pageant. Katy sang "Firework" at the MTV Europe Music Awards with a live fireworks display. "Firework" was the last song that Katy recorded for her *Teenage Dream* album. It was also Katy's favorite song from the album.

The song "Circle the Drain" is one of Katy's darker songs and deals with her relationship with an ex-boyfriend who she believed was keeping her down with his attitude and outlook on life. The lyrics of "Circle the Drain" have been described as being like an emotional colonic—if you know something is not right with a relationship then you have to know when to move on. The title refers to getting sucked into the drain with someone and all his or her life's drama. Many have speculated that this song was written about Katy's ex-boyfriend Travis McCoy, but Katy has never said exactly who the song refers to. McCoy downplayed that the song was written with him in mind. In an interview with *MTV News,* he stated, "I heard that she put out a song about me, or about some old habits or whatever. I look at it like this: I'm just stoked that she finally has a song with some substance on her record. Good job."[6] "Hot N Cold" is also about a relationship that Katy had with a moody man.

The upbeat "Teenage Dream" song refers to the feeling of euphoria people get when they fall in love for the first time. Teenagers are always on the lookout for that one person who makes them feel special. Katy traveled to her hometown of Santa Barbara to write "Teenage Dream," as she thought Los Angeles was just too noisy and too busy for her to get the song written there. Santa Barbara was where it all began for Katy when she sang in the choir in high school and where she developed her own teenage dream of becoming a musician and a singer. The song was rewritten at least five times over the course of 10 days.

The music video for "E.T." was one of the most singular of all Katy's videos. It featured singer Kanye West along with futuristic special effects. Katy appears as an alien in the video; the process of making her an alien figure took five or six hours to achieve the look the make-up artists and producers wanted. Katy had to remain patient while they transformed her into an alien. Despite the long, grueling hours it took to put her face on, the whole removal process took only about 10 minutes.

In late 2010, Katy's single "Part of Me" was leaked onto the Internet. Despite the fact that Katy was happily married to Brand, she poured her heart into the break-up song "Part of Me." The song was written with Dr. Luke and Max Martin. The song was about a relationship that Katy was involved in that ended up in her boyfriend breaking up with her. In the song she sings about how even after being heart broken she was able to keep her identity.

"Last Friday Night (T.G.I.F)" is a song about a teenager who tries to remember what happened at a party she threw on a Friday night when her parents were away at a convention. The video shows Kathy Beth Terry, actually portrayed by Katy, singing about what happened and reliving the events of the night with a video someone taped. The video features the boy band Hanson and saxophonist Kenny G. Kathy Beth Terry's parents are played by '80s stars Corey Feldman and Debbie Gibson. Darren Criss of *Glee* fame portrays one of the hunks in the clip. The video was released on June 14, 2011. Kenny G. appeared in the video to acquaint himself with a new generation of fans. He was excited that younger people recognized him from the video. In an interview with the *Boston Herald,* Kenny G. said, "That was the big one. It's really, really cool because I wasn't on the teenage radar (before). Everyone needs to reinvent themselves today."[7] Many artists collaborate and do videos to expose themselves to new listeners. The invention of YouTube and Facebook has made it possible for people to retrieve videos and songs without having to go to a concert or to buy a CD. Hanson, the three-brother band, was formed in 1997 and made their big break with the song "MMMBop." The group was flattered that they were asked by one of pop culture's favorite musicians to be in their video. They thought it was different than anything they had done in the past. As the house band in the video, they were featured on the lawn playing to a bunch of rowdy teenagers. During down times and breaks during the filming of the video, the band entertained themselves and the extras on the set. Hanson also enjoyed working with Kenny G. during the video because they realized that Kenny G. is a music icon. They were also amazed at Katy's alter-ego, Kathy Beth Terry, and how Katy played the part so well on the set. After the band so graciously and enthusiastically performed in her video, Katy said she would not be opposed to making a cameo performance in one of the Hanson brothers' videos.

"Last Friday Night (T.G.I.F)" was also in the running in 2011 as the VH1 Song of the Summer. Although "Last Friday Night (T.G.I.F)" did not fare as well on the charts as Katy's previous 2010 Song of the Summer "California Gurls," its catchy tune had radio listeners singing along. LMAFO's song, "Party Anthem," was also vying for the title of 2011 Song of the Summer. The songs that are nominated for the Song of the Summer are those that a person can roll down their windows and sing out loud to. "Last Friday Night (T.G.I.F.)" received the accolade of VH1's 2011 Song of the Summer. Adele's song "Rolling in the Deep" was ranked at number two. The top 10 artists, according to the poll, included Katy, Adele, LMFAO, Bruno Mars, Ne-Yo, Lady Gaga, Britney Spears, Jennifer Lopez, Foster the People, and Hot Chelle Rae. The artists were compiled from five different popular lists, including the Billboard Hot 100, iTunes sales, Last.fm downloads on computers and mobile devices, YouTube streams, and the VH1 Top 20 Video Countdown.

Before the release of the *Teenage Dream* album, Katy gave concerts and played many of the tracks from the album to entice her fans into purchasing and downloading the album and its songs. Katy admitted that although some of the songs on the album were full of substance, there were some, like "Last Friday Night (T.G.I.F.)," that were done for fun and were just catchy tunes that people could sing along with. She did the beach-party-themed parties to see her fans having fun and to see first-hand the emotions that her songs had on her fans.

The *Teenage Dream* album contained both pop songs and ballads, with songs written by Dr. Luke, Max Martin, Trickey Stewart, and Stargate. Unfortunately, many critics found the songs robotic, containing nothing new from what Katy had produced on her first pop album. The album was given one star out of four on the Amazon Web site.

The album was released on August 24, 2010. In its first week the album sold more than 192,000 copies. The album cover featured Katy naked on the cover lying on a cloud with cotton candy covering her rear end. The booklet inside the album, which features the credits and songs, was sprayed with candy floss to tie in with the cotton candy on the cover. In 2011, *Teenage Dream* reached platinum status with more than one million copies sold. Katy became the "10th solo female in the Hot 100's 52-year history to concurrently place two titles in the top five of the list."[8] By the end of the summer of 2011, *Teenage Dream* had brought in $50 million in record sales and sold 1.7 million copies. Twenty million single tracks had been purchased. "With albums retailing for roughly $13 and singles for $1.30, her financial partners will share more than $48 million, minus marketing and retailers' share."[9] The success that Katy has achieved entitles her to between 15 and 20 percent of all music revenues. Monetarily and popularly, Katy has garnered success as defined by the music industry, based on her album sales and Internet downloads. Katy used Twitter to find out from her fans which tracks from her albums should be released and in what order.

Katy loaned her vocals to Selena Gomez's album, *A Year Without Rain*, in 2010. Gomez was also thought to have Miley Cyrus and Demi Lovato contribute to the album as well, but it turned out to only be Katy. Katy gave Gomez the song, "Rock God," a song about choosing rock and roll over religion. Gomez and Katy were paired together because Gomez enjoyed Katy's style and enthusiasm in her songs. The two also shared the same music agent.

Katy began the *California Dreams* tour in February 2011. It was a tour that went through 41 cities in nine months. The concert began in Lisbon, Portugal, and ended in Dublin, Ireland, in November 2011. The entourage included 12 semis, 8 buses, 37 tons of gear, and 44 crew members. The production manager was Jay Schmit. The director was Baz Halpin, who had been Lady Gaga's director for her latest tour. The stage was decorated in a Candyland theme. At one point Katy turned into Kitty Purry, wearing a cat jumpsuit. She had 15 costume changes in all during the show. The concert began with Katy floating on a cloud strumming a guitar. The tour featured an *Alice in Wonderland*-type theme. It involved Katy's escape from an evil butcher and Katy trying to find her true love. Each song during the performance had its own production that included different sets, dancers, costumes, and videos. Katy's costume changes were able to be done on stage due to some optical illusions.

The tour used smell-o-vision so everything smelled like cotton candy. Katy was excited about putting this feature into her tour because it was something that musicians usually do not use. In an interview with *Rolling Stone* magazine, Katy said, "It's the first concert that's going to smell good. It's going to smell like you are in cotton candy heaven. It's a fun little nuance. I am a woman of detail, and you will be seeing that—even down to the 15 outfit changes I'm doing in concert."[10]

Katy made an impromptu appearance at the Melbourne High School prom when she was in Australia for a concert. The prom took place at the same hotel that Katy was staying in. Katy heard "California Gurls" playing at the dance and decided to grab a microphone and sing the song for real. It was also reported that she sang and danced with students to Beyoncé's hit "Single Ladies." Katy stayed at the prom for only 10 minutes, but tweeted after that that she crashed a prom party.

Katy gave fans her all during the *California Dreams* tour. Katy was enthralled by her audience's emotions during each concert. She loved seeing the crowd dancing and responding positively to her music. In each city in the United States she stopped in, she was greeted warmly by her fans. Music has helped Katy get through difficulties in her life. She envisions herself as an inspiration to produce music that people can relate to and to get her fans through their tough times.

Artist Will Cotton decorated the sets and also provided the cover art for the *Teenage Dream* album cover. Cotton, in turn, asked Katy to appear in his art exhibit in Los Angeles. The exhibit that Cotton asked Katy to appear in, along with other models, portrayed candy-covered "royalty" and he made crowns for his subjects. He has worked with Katy in the past and knows that a model's personality shines when she is wearing the right clothes. Many of Cotton's works paint a candy-colored world, and Katy was flattered to be in his exhibit. Cotton said, "There's something about her look that coincided with what I was doing. She wanted to ask me if it was OK to work with her. That was good for me, for sure. It made me feel much better about doing stuff with her. She seemed to get what I was doing."[11] Cotton was unsure in the beginning to even ask Katy to pose for his exhibit because he does not make it a habit of asking pop stars that he was working with to be in his art exhibits. With Katy though, their styles seemed to match.

At the August 2011 concert at the Nokia Theater in Los Angeles, Katy brought up fellow singer Rebecca Black to sing with her onstage. Katy has helped Black throughout her short career by including Black in her videos and praising Black's work and energy in the press. The two sang the chorus of Black's hot song "Friday," which received more than a million hits on YouTube when it was first released. The crowd at the concert amassed more than 7,000 people. Katy also performed songs by Whitney Houston and Jay-Z.

Katy made it through her performance at Summerfest in Milwaukee, but she was feeling a bit under the weather. After consulting with a doctor, it was found that Katy was suffering not only from food poisoning but also from severe dehydration. Katy had to cancel shows in the Midwest because of this; she rescheduled shows in both Chicago and Minneapolis. When she did perform the shows in the two cities later in the summer, Katy apologized for her absence and need to cancel the shows. Katy also had to postpone her Grand Rapids, Michigan, performance because she had an upper respiratory tract infection. Singer Janelle Monae was to be the opening act for the concert. The September 11, 2011, concert was postponed until December 1, 2011. Those fans who had tickets were told they could be refunded or their tickets would be honored at the December concert. At her Columbus, Ohio, concert, Katy was fighting off a cold but did not let it hamper her performance in any way. During the concert, she did mention her malady and said that because of her cold she would just sing louder. Part of Katy's act includes interacting and chatting with the audience. She mentioned her bike ride around Columbus with Brand and also her affection for a local ice cream store. Fans were singing along to the lyrics and Katy also kissed a 15-year-old fan in the audience. Katy closed the concert with her lively tunes "Last Friday Night (T.G.I.F.)" and her signature "Firework" song, complete with pyrotechnics. After the concert, many of the fans in attendance tweeted their support and enthusiasm for Katy, despite her having been under the weather. They affectionately labeled the topic "Columbus Dreams."

During the show at the Scott Trade Center in St. Louis, Katy talked about the Golden Arch. She also took the time when she was not performing to bicycle around the city giving tickets to people. Janelle Monae opened for Katy at the St. Louis show. She sang "Tightrope," "Cold War," and "Come Alive" from her album The ArchAndroid. Monae also did a rendition of the Jackson 5 song "I Want You Back." When Katy went to Nashville to perform at the Bridgestone Arena she felt right at home. She mentioned things that only people who lived in Nashville could relate to, such as the Pancake Pantry, Tootsies, and Jack's Bar-B-Que. She also reminisced about staying at the AmeriSuites hotel in Franklin when she was writing her gospel songs and trying to sell her album early in her career. There were some celebrities in the crowd whose presence made Katy nervous, including

Reba McEntire and Faith Hill. She gratified the audience when she told them, despite her success and how big she has gotten in the past few years, that she enjoys being close to her fans and feeling their energy. Katy is a grounded musician and always remembers that her fans are those that made her successful.

The repertoire of songs on the tour boasted 20 singles, including "Teenage Dream," "Hummingbird Heartbeat," "Waking Up in Vegas," "Ur So Gay," "Peacock," "I Kissed a Girl," "Circle the Drain," "E.T.," "Who Am I Living For?" "Pearl," "Not Like the Movies," Rihanna's "Only Girl (in the World)," Jay-Z's "Big Pimpin," Rebecca Black's "Friday," Willow Smith's "Whip My Hair," "Thinking of You," "Hot N Cold," "Last Friday Night (T.G.I.F.)," "I Wanna Dance with Somebody," and "Firework." Katy saves her song "California Gurls" for when she is asked to do an encore presentation. The shows on tour were two hours of candy-filled fun. Each song required its own set, which made for many set and costume changes. There was a pre-show mini-movie that was playing throughout the show.

The press that accompanied the concerts was positive about the energy and creativeness of the concerts. Tulsa, Oklahoma, was the last American stop on Katy's *California Dreams* Tour. She told the crowd that Tulsa had a special place in her heart because her brother David was born there and attended the Rhema Bible Training Center, and some of her first memories were of Tulsa. The movie clip that played during the whole concert featured cats, a butcher cutting up beef, and cupcakes. Her rendition of the songs "Hot N Cold" and "Last Friday Night (T.G.I.F)" had the whole audience dancing. Katy gets her energy for her concerts through her fans who are dancing and singing her songs in the crowd. She brought onstage approximately 20 audience members to help her sing along to Whitney Houston's "I Wanna Dance with Somebody." The concert ended with Katy singing "Firework," complete with fireworks. For her encore, she sang one of her top number one hits, "California Gurls."

Such artists as Ellie Goulding performed with Katy on the tour. Goulding joined Katy for her concerts in Hartford, New York, Oakland, Las Vegas, and Los Angeles. Goulding replaced Jessie J, who was recovering from and receiving physical therapy for an injury. Jessie J cried when she found out doctors would not give her the okay to tour with Katy. Earlier in 2011, Jessie J had to cancel concerts after having a bone transplant in her left foot. She fell earlier in the year and broke her foot in two places. She cancelled appearances at the T in the Park Festival, Lovebox, and the iTunes Festival.

Katy trained very hard for the *California Dreams* tour, both physically and vocally. She could direct more energy to the tour since her love life was not up in the air and she was happily married. Training for the tour was much like training for the Olympics. Her days consisted of eating breakfast, having a vocal lesson, rehearsing an entire set of the concert, going to dance rehearsals to get the choreography right, and, finally, sifting through e-mails about the concert and the direction it was going—then she went to bed and started it all over again in the morning. Because Katy's days are filled when she is on tour, she has said that when a tour ends she feels a little lost. On tour she always has people who take her places, who plan when and what she eats, and who plan her agenda for the day. After the whirlwind tours end, Katy is left making the decisions by herself. Although she does not have a problem making her own decisions, she sometimes finds it easier on tour.

Katy admitted to being a perfectionist and having some obsessive compulsive tendencies in an interview with *Q* magazine. Katy said she too has certain things that send her over the edge, most specifically, if there are fingerprints on her sunglasses. Katy claimed that her condition worsens when she is on tour because things are always happening that interfere with her routine. She also wants everything to go smoothly and perfectly for her fans when she is on tour.

Katy's career has been a roller coaster from the beginning, with the disappointment of being dropped by many record labels to having two platinum selling albums and several number one hits. In 2011 she tied Michael Jackson's record of having five number one hit singles from the same album. Jackson had five singles from his album *Bad* reach number one. "Last Friday Night (T.G.I.F.)," "California Gurls," "E.T.," "Firework," and "Teenage Dream" have all soared to the top of the charts. However, Jackson's top hits only stayed in the Top 100 for seven weeks whereas Katy's songs remained at the top of the charts for 18 consecutive weeks. She has actually had seven chart-topping hits. Aside from the five from her *Teenage Dream* album, "Hot N Cold" and

"Waking Up in Vegas," from her *One of the Boys* album, also climbed to the top of the charts. Lady Gaga, Pink, and Katy are in a three-way tie for having the second most number ones in the charts; Rihanna has eight number one singles in the Billboard chart archives. More than four million copies of each of Katy's hits had sold by the middle of 2011 for her singles "E.T," "California Gurls," "Firework," "Hot N Cold," and "I Kissed a Girl." Katy's song went for a record-breaking 48 consecutive weeks on the Top 10, beating the previous record holder, Ace of Base. Katy has also "become the first artist in US chart history to spend an entire year in the top 10."[12] In 2011, she released her sixth single from the album, "The One That Got Away."

Katy Perry is also the only artist in the history of the Video Music Awards to be nominated for four separate videos in one year. In 2011 she was nominated for nine MTV Video Music Awards—a testament to her hard work and determination. The nominations were announced in a live television presentation on July 20, 2011. Katy expressed her elation when she was interviewed during the

At the 39th Annual American Music Awards in 2011 in Los Angeles, Katy performs her song "The One that Got Away." She was presented with a Special Achievement Award. (AP Photo/Matt Sayles.)

nominations. She said, "Nine? I thought that was a typo or something! Oh my god, really? That's the most nominations I've ever gotten for anything."[13] Nominations at that time for her videos included Video of the Year for "Firework"; Best Female Video for "Firework"; Best Pop Video for "Last Friday Night (T.G.I.F.)"; Best Collaboration for "E.T."; Best Art Direction for "E.T."; Best Direction for "E.T."; Best Editing for "E.T."; Best Special Effects for "E.T."; and Best Cinematography for the video "Teenage Dream." Other nominees included Lady Gaga, Adele, Britney Spears, and Nicki Minaj. Of the nine Video Music Awards, Katy brought home three of them. She won Video of the Year for "Firework," Best Collaboration for "E.T." with Kanye West, and Best Special Effects for "E.T." At the awards ceremony, Katy and Kanye West together accepted the Moonman for Best Collaboration. The two hugged and thanked the director of the video "E.T." The video beat out Chris Brown's "Look at Me Now," Kanye West's "All of the Lights," Pitbull's "Give Me Everything," and Nicki Minaj's "Moment 4 Life."

Katy was also nominated for four MTV European Music Awards, including Best Song for "Firework," Best Live Performance, Best Female, and Best Pop. Katy was nominated in these four categories against pop-culture icon Lady Gaga, who had six MTV Europe Music Award nominations. The awards took place on November 6, 2011, at Odyssey Arena in Belfast, Ireland. Katy was nominated for two BT Digital Music Awards in September 2011; one for Artist of the Year, which is determined by judges; and Best International Award, which is voted on by the public via a Web site.

In her own unique style, Katy planned her next album around meat, seeing as her first album was fruit-themed and her second album was candy-themed. During 2010 and 2011 she had been exercising intensely to get ready for her *California Dreams* tour, and it took a lot out of her physically. She also stuck to a very stringent diet. She has tried to become a vegetarian like her husband Brand, but that has not worked for Katy. She commented, "For my next album I'd like it to be about meat and I want to be on the cover wearing a bacon bikini. Also I want my records to smell of sausage or pork. CDs are over, but not if they smell original."[14]

Katy's music career catapulted after she signed with Capitol Records. She was given creative license to develop new songs and express her style through her concerts and costumes. She continually promotes her songs and entertains with her concert tours. Ian Drew, the senior music director at *Us Weekly* commented, "Even though it's a year old, this album is proving to be one big greatest-hits party."[15] Katy has proven her staying power as her songs remain on the music charts.

NOTES

1. Carissa Rosenberg, "Katy Perry," *Seventeen Magazine*, September 2010, p. 194.

2. Jo Berry, *Katy Perry California Gurl* (London: Orion Publishing Group, 2011), p. 80.

3. Askshay Bhansali, "Katy Perry Is Jealous of Taylor Swift's Part in VMA Promo," *MTV News*, August 17, 2009. www.mtvnews.com.

4. Anne Brown, *Katy Perry*, People in the News Series (New York: Lucent Books, 2011), p. 59.

5. Jocelyn Vena, "How Katy Perry Avoided a Sophomore Slump," *MTV News*, December 30, 2010. www.mtvnews.com.

6. James C. Montgomery, Travie McCoy Finally Addresses Katy Perry's 'Circle the Drain'," *MTV News*, October 1, 2010. www.mtvnews.com.

7. Chris Epting, "Todd Rundgren Dismisses Pop Acts Like Katy Perry, Rihanna Over Focus on Innuendo, Not 'Messages'," *AOL News*, September 15, 2011. www.aolnews.com.

8. Gary Trust, "Eminem Rihanna Top Hot 100 for Fifth Week," *Billboard*, August 19, 2010. www.billboard.com.

9. Claire Atkinson, "Katy Perry Takes Crown as No. 1 'Dream' Queen," *New York Post*, August 18, 2011. www.nypost.com.

10. Andy Greene, "Katy Reveals Plans for California Dreams World Tour," *Rolling Stone Magazine*, January 27, 2011. www.rollingstone.com.

11. Jocelyn Vena, "Katy Perry Featured in New Will Cotton Exhibit," *MTV News*, January 14, 2011. www.mtvnews.com.

12. "Katy Perry Breaks US Billboard Chart Record," *BBC News*, May 17, 2011. www.bbc.co.uk.

13. Jocelyn Vena, "Katy Perry 'So Excited' About Nine VMA Nods," *MTV News*, July 21, 2011. www.mtvnews.com.

14. "Lady Gaga Wears a Red Meat Bikini," *Rising Stars*, September 7, 2010. www.risingstarstv.net.

15. Marco R. della Cava, "Katy Perry Is One Hit Away from a Broken Record," *USA Today*, August 18, 2011. www.usatoday.com.

Chapter 4

A STYLE OF MY OWN

Katy Perry's dress and musical style are other characteristics that define her as a popular entertainer. The very fact that she tries to stand out from the crowd and entertain her followers with her flamboyant costumes and theatrics is a large part of why Katy is successful as a performer. According to creative consultant and designer Todd Thomas, who designs many of Katy's costumes and is the designer on the Victoria's Secret Fashion Show, said, "She has a very clear vision of how she wants to portray herself, and the energy surrounding her is very different from anything I've ever experienced before. That's why I think she is a success now."[1]

That vision of what she wanted to become started out in her early formative years. During her childhood Katy would go through stages where she would change up her style of dress. Her mother reminisces that Katy would come down in a different outfit for breakfast, lunch, and dinner. When she took swing dance lessons at the age of 13, she changed her style of dress to rockabilly. Her teachers at her Santa Barbara dance school greatly influenced her fashion choices. She learned how to swing, lindy, hop, and jitterbug while wearing pencil skirts, tight cardigans, and bullet bras. During her punk rock stage she

Katy traveled to Milan for the D&G Spring/Summer fashion show on September 22, 2008. (AP Photo/Alberto Pellaschiar.)

wore jeans that she would draw on and T-shirts with logos, pictures, and sayings on them. In the 1990s she changed her hair to a pixie cut with barrettes. Katy was not always comfortable with the way she looked. She always thought her chest was too big so she would wear a minimizer bra when she was younger, but then people made fun of her, laughing at her "over-the-shoulder boulder-holder." She became more comfortable with her figure when she realized it would make people notice her and her quirky style.

Katy's overall style and music lyrics have categorized her with other singers like Rihanna, Lady Gaga, and Fergie, whose costumes and lyrics have placed them into a new generation of pop stars. Katy has also been compared to '80s superstar Madonna. Madonna also had a religious upbringing, although was brought up in the Catholic faith, and is known for her rebellious side. Madonna has commented in the media that she endorses Katy and cites "Ur So Gay" as one of her favorite songs. Madonna mentioned the song on Phoenix's 104.7 KISS FM JohnJay & Rich morning show. She also spoke of the song again on Ryan Seacrest's Morning show. The two singers met in 2008 when Madonna invited Katy to one of her shows and wanted to meet her backstage. Katy had butterflies in her stomach and nearly threw up upon meeting the celebrity icon. When Katy met Madonna the only words she could muster to say to the mega star were "Thank you." Madonna had an entourage of her close friends and her dancers with her when she and Katy met.

Many of Katy's hair and clothing styles date back to the 1950s and 1960s and can be described as "pin-up model" styles. As a teenager she would sneak into Universal Studios in Los Angeles and pretend that she was a stylist. She would then try on all the different dresses and ball gowns. Jane Russell, a celebrity symbol of the '40s and '50s, was a friend of the Hudson family and was a great influence on Katy. Although Katy's major influences were from the '50s and '60s, Katy said she gets her style ideas from many different avenues. In an interview with *Scarlet* magazine, Katy described her look. "I'm not strictly 1940s pin-up girl—I don't have that kind of dedication—so I gave it a little twist. It's a little punk rock, a little Lolita, a little retro, a little Eighties. Just fun. It makes people smile I think."[2]

Katy had started wearing Wolford neon tights because she liked the way they looked on fellow musician Beyoncé. Her elaborate outfits are stored in a large container in a secret location.

Katy's make-up style also comes from influences of pop culture, even though she was not exposed to it in her childhood. She started developing her own fashion style while she was in Nashville. She changed her hair color from sandy brown to the dark brunette it is today. However, Katy has been pictured in not just the black hair color, but also pink, blue, and purple as well. "I've been glued to the TV watching Liza [Minnelli]'s song and dance numbers. So I've picked up my make-up tips from her and got that overall 1930s dark romantic style."[3] During an episode of *MTV Hoods*, Katy was taken back to the theater to reminisce about her days on the stage. On the show Katy claimed that it was in the theater that she actually began applying heavy make-up, both on her eyes and on her lips. This is where she started making herself look like a geisha. The geisha look comes from Katy's love of the Japanese culture. She was first influenced by the Japanese culture when her parents opened up their house to Japanese exchange students. At the Japanese MTV Video Music Awards she wore a leotard embroidered with pieces of sushi.

The official word for making Katy up in her costumes and in her full make-up before her concerts is called "Glam." Katy's make-up artist is Todd Delano. Some of the costume changes for her tours have been very elaborate and extensive. At the 2008 MTV Europe Music Awards in Liverpool, England, Katy did 12 costume changes. She began the night in a football uniform and was on stage with a huge ChapStick to represent her lyrics to "I Kissed a Girl." During the show she also wore a full skirt alive with carnival colors. The night ended with Katy singing "Hot N Cold," donning a half tuxedo/half wedding-dress outfit. The 2008 MTV Music Awards saw her paying tribute to President Barack Obama. She wore a yellow sequined dress with Obama's face on it.

While her first album did have a fruity theme, she also used that theme in her costumes and performances to present awards and while she was on tour. At the 2009 Grammy Awards, she came onstage with a sparkly banana and wearing artificial fruit and sequins. According to Katy, "I have multipersonality disorder—in a very good way, of course—when it comes to my fashion choices."[4] Although Katy likes her clothes to be flashy and entertaining, she also likes her wardrobe to be comfortable and accessible. At a May 4, 2010 concert, Katy wore a pink gown complete with LED lights.

During the Teenage Choice Awards in August 2010, Katy changed her outfit a total of four times during the presentations. Katy headlined the awards by singing "Teenage Dream" and was dressed as a cheerleader. She even managed to do the splits in the opening number. She appeared as a hippie in one number. While she was on stage with Mark Salling, who is an actor on *Glee*, she appeared as Kathy Beth Terry, complete with braces, headgear, and large, taped glasses. In another act, with Chris Colfer, who is also an actor on *Glee*, Katy wore a prom dress with a prom queen sash and a tiara. Katy won Best Single and Best Summer song for "California Gurls" with Snoop Dogg.

Katy's second album had a candy theme so she changed her costumes in her concerts and appearances to reflect this. When she performed on the season opener of *Saturday Night Live* on September 25, 2010, she was wearing a dress covered with candy beads and was sporting a pair of red and white stripped boots. She wore a red dress resembling a movie ticket for the 2010 MTV Europe Music Awards. The dress she wore to the 2010 Met Institute Costume Gala was twinkling like a Christmas tree and the 2010 Jingle Ball concert had her in a three-dimensional snowman dress. At one of her concerts, she had a bra made out of whipped-cream cans that actually squirted whipped cream. These crazy antics have fans clamoring for more of Katy and her whimsical style. Part of Katy's appeal is the entertainment value of her concerts, and fans are just waiting for what Katy has in store for them next.

On the *California Dreams* Tour in 2011, the show included bubbles, lasers, and cotton candy scents. The lasers were used during the song "Not Like the Movies." During the song "Hot N Cold," Katy changed her outfit eight times. Many musicians and singers are putting more energy into making their concerts theatrical shows with elaborate costumes and props.

Despite her need to entertain her fans with her shows, Katy also likes to be comfortable. She likes to garage sale shop and visit thrift stores. This is a tradition that her father started when she was eight years old. The duo would go to thrift stores and garage sales on Saturday mornings. Even when she is on tour, Katy makes it a point to take a day to shop the vintage and antiques stores wherever she is.

Katy also used topics in the news to decide on her style of the moment. Katy showed her royal spirit for the wedding of Prince William and Kate Middleton by getting a manicure with pictures of the couple on all 10 of her fingernails. One of the pictures was of Prince William as a baby being held by the late Princess Diana. There was also a picture of both Prince William and Prince Harry, who was the best man. Katy posted a picture of her manicure for all the world to see on Facebook and Twitter. Katy's love of Great Britain and the Royal Family blossomed after she married British actor Brand.

Because she has so many fans and is exposed to so many people, designers send Katy free clothes because they know their fashions will then be exposed to a lot of people. Designer Betsy Johnson sends

Katy free clothes. Many of Katy's flamboyant costumes are designed by David and Phillipe Blond, who have also made fashions for Rihanna, Adam Lambert, and Fergie of The Black Eyed Peas.

The Blonds started their label in 2004 and became fashion-designer legends when celebrities began to don their outlandish outfits. They have been incorrectly labeled as costume designers but even though most of their fashions are outrageous, they can still be worn in public at premieres and performances. The vision behind the Blonds designs is that they provide fashion as escapism for celebrities.

Not only do her costumes entertain fans, her lyrics have also caused jaw dropping among the public and her adorers. Her lyrics are based on emotional and real-life experiences. As her album covers carry themes, her songs do as well. Katy "is aware that some people are shocked or put off by the content of a few of her songs,"[5] but this does not stop Katy from producing what is in her heart.

In her music and in her personal life Katy likes to have fun and likes to make people smile. She keeps her crew happy on tour by taking them to dinner and the movies. She has "slumber parties" on her tour bus for the musicians and the dancers. Many times they wear their pajamas and watch movies. Katy has a following of groupies called the Katy Cats who come to all her shows. In every online poll, Katy makes it a point to thank the Katy Cats for all their hard work in helping her to earn her awards. As a musician, Katy knows that her groupies are an important part of her concerts and performances. Her wardrobe choices, videos, and entertaining concerts are so much more than a musician creating a song and singing it. According to author Jo Berry, "her own vibrant stage costumes, outrageous concert performances, and clever, fun music videos are a tribute to the artist who so bewitched a teenage California girl."[6]

At the MTV Video Music Awards in 2011, Katy revealed lavender-colored locks. It is not shocking to the public any more what color Katy's hair is. Many times she changes her looks to reflect a costume she is wearing or a song she is singing. She achieved this color with the help of New York salon owner Rita Hazan. Hazan liked working with Katy because Katy liked doing different things and wasn't afraid to experiment. Hazan said, "It was such an exciting challenge to custom-create Katy's color for her big reveal at the VMAs. She is a colorist's dream —always willing to take risks to achieve a groundbreaking look—and it was awesome to be able to realize this goal for her."[7] She is constantly changing her hair color to stay different. Before sporting lavender, she experimented with blond and pink. True to form, Katy changed her outfit four times during the Video Music Awards. Her first outfit was a Versace geisha dress complete with a parasol. When she introduced singer Adele she was in outfit number two, a floor-length purple gown by Tom Ford, which accentuated her hair. The third outfit, a black minidress adorned with vinyl records, was more the outlandish style people expect from Katy. When she accepted her Video of the Year Award, she was wearing her fourth outfit. Atop her head was a cube-style hat and she wore a pink top with a black and white tulip skirt. The outfit was topped off with neon-colored platform shoes.

Katy has enjoyed hosting and performing at the Video Music Awards (VMA) and thinks it is the most fun of all the award shows she has participated in. The 2011 VMA Award show included Lady Gage dressed as a man, Beyoncé announcing to the public that she was expecting a baby, and Chris Brown flying in on wires. Romance also has abounded at the awards. It is where Katy and Brand started their courtship and where young loves Justin Bieber and Selena Gomez shared a kiss. Every year something out of the ordinary happens at the VMA awards.

Katy also takes her style choices from other models and singers. On the June 2011 cover of *Vanity Fair*, Katy looked strikingly similar to Dita von Teese when she attended a WonderBra presentation in London. The two looked stunning, with pin-up-style curls, a strapless cream-colored dress, and bright-red-colored nail polish. Von Teese was not upset about the imitation. She was flattered and saw the cover of *Vanity Fair* as a compliment. In an interview with *Entertainment Online*, von Teese stated, "Katy and I are friends. She comes to a lot of my shows, but she came backstage and said, 'I am taking all of this (gesturing at her hair and costume)'."[8]

Katy tries not to let her success go to her head and is often described as an outrageous but down-to-earth person. In an interview with *Fabulous Magazine* out of the United Kingdom, Katy said, "I say what I think. I'm a real person, not some manufactured pop tart who's afraid to step out of the hotel room. I am flawed. I swear, I have the occasional cocktail, I pick my nose and I fart. I'm not running for any presidential campaign at the moment. I'm a sassy girl."[9] She gives autographs to fans after her concerts. However, despite being good to her fans, she does have a celebrity contract rider for her chauffeurs. The rider says that the chauffeurs must not make eye contact with Katy or request autographs from Katy. The chauffeur rider also states that drivers are not to stare at Katy through the rear view mirror. There are 23 parts to the document, with an important part being that drivers are not to initiate conversations with celebrities.

Many celebrities have specific requests of what they want backstage while they are on tour. Katy asks for a refrigerator with a glass door, crème-colored chairs, and hydrangeas, roses, and peonies in her flower arrangements. Katy does not allow carnations in her flower mix.

Facebook and Twitter have given celebrities the ability to let fans know what they are doing every minute of the day. Katy created a persona called Kathy Beth Terry who supposedly is Katy's biggest fan. Kathy Beth Terry appears in the video "Last Friday Night (T.G.I.F.)." She has braces and glasses and tells fans of her latest adventures. Kathy Beth Terry is portrayed as a 13-year-old girl who is trying to fit in. T.G.I.F. comes from the popular ABC block of Friday night shows in the 90s, which coincidentally included the fictional character Steve Urkel, whom Kathy Beth Terry resembles in the nerd department. Kathy Beth Terry seems to be an Internet fascination. She has more than 67,000 Facebook friends and more than 20,000 followers on Twitter. Kathy Beth Terry's birthdate is listed as June 1, 1998, on Facebook. She has even filled in her interests, which are evident in the video and include science fairs, Beanie Babies, and the pop group Hanson.

Katy used to Google herself to find the latest news about herself and what critics have said about her latest releases. However, when she found out that Brand was going to propose in 2009, she realized that googling herself was not a good idea. She made a New Year's resolution in 2011 to stop searching for herself on the Internet. Despite not googling herself anymore, Katy does work on her Web site and also tweets. She has more than nine million followers on Twitter.

Katy has used material from pop culture when she was growing up, even though she herself was never exposed to it. The comical approach to her music and style keeps fans wanting more. "Katy describes her approach as somewhere between Lucille Ball—the great American TV comedienne of the 1950s and '60s—and Freddie Mercury, who she described as 'pretty much my biggest influence and idol'."[10]

NOTES

1. April Long, "Fantastic Voyage," *Elle*, March 2011, p. 403.

2. Jo Berry, *Katy Perry California Gurl* (London: Orion Publishing Group, 2011), p. 127.

3. Dave Stone, *Russell Brand and Katy Perry: The Love Story* (London: John Blake Publishing, 2010), p. 299.

4. Rose Apodaca, "What Katy Perry Did Next," *Harper's Bazaar*, December 2010, p. 286.

5. Leah Greenblatt, " 'Girl' On Top." *Entertainment Weekly*, August 1, 2008, p. 29.

6. Jo Berry, *Katy Perry California Gurl*, p. 26.

7. Gina Serpe, "Katy Perry-Russell Brand Cheating Claim—Katy (and the Truth) Poke Holes in Report," *Entertainment Online*, April 28, 2011. www.eonline.com.

8. Ella Stewart, Bitch Stole My Look: Katy Perry vs. Dita Von Teese," *Entertainment Online*, May 9, 2011. www.eonline.com.

9. "Katy Perry Is the Real Deal," *Fabulous Magazine*, December 2008. www.fabulousmag.co.uk.

10. David Stone, *Russell Brand and Katy Perry: The Love Story*, p. 245.

Chapter 5

"ONE OF THE BOYS"

Katy has prided herself in only having had five relationships with men. She believes in looking for that one special person. She does admit to being attracted to difficult, creative types of men. Unfortunately, as a celebrity Katy has to be careful whom she dates and what she does for fear of what the press reports about her personal life.

Katy's first publicized relationship after putting out her first album was with musician Travis "Travie" McCoy of the alternative, hip-hop band Gym Class Heroes. Katy appeared in the band's video for their song "Cupid's Chokehold." The two actually met in a recording studio in New York in 2006. McCoy liked Katy but thought the best way to get her attention would be to ignore her. The juvenile antics worked and the two began dating. At the beginning of the Warped Tour in 2008, in which both Katy and McCoy participated, the two were considered a serious couple. McCoy had given Katy a promise ring and he wore a silver band with the name Katy engraved on it. When McCoy presented Katy with the ring, he was scared. He put flowers everywhere to create the right atmosphere. He felt more comfortable when Katy's reaction was so positively enthusiastic. McCoy was supportive in the press of Katy when she released "I Kissed a Girl" and the song soared to number one on iTunes. He expressed that she had been in the music business for more than six years and she finally got the well-deserved break she was entitled to.

Through the relationship, Katy helped McCoy battle with depression. In 2008, McCoy checked himself into a rehabilitation center to work on his addiction to pharmaceutical drugs. Katy and McCoy split up in December 2008 while on a trip to Mexico. The two were seen back together in May 2009. They attended the Life Ball in Vienna, Austria, a charity event that supports and raises money for HIV/AIDS. Later in 2009, the couple broke up again. Travis McCoy's song "Don't Pretend" is about he and Katy's tumultuous relationship. In the media, McCoy expressed no ill feelings toward Katy. He said in the press that his former girlfriend, referring to Katy, saved his life. When he and Katy dated, he was at a low point in his life, suffering from depression and low self-esteem. McCoy explained that Katy just listened to him and that in itself helped him a great deal. After Katy and McCoy broke up, Katy vowed that the only thing that she would be kissing would be her cat, Kitty Purry. Katy made some general remarks at a concert, which she often does to build a rapport with her audience, but some took the remarks out of context, relating them directly to her break up with McCoy. Katy did not want her personal life played out in the press and in the public. Katy put all her energies and focus on the *Hello Katy* tour when the two split up.

In 2009, there were rumors that Katy was dating singer Josh Groban. Perez Hilton reported that the two were in a relationship but strived to keep the courtship as low-profile as possible. After Katy's break up with McCoy, she was rumored to have been seeing many people, including Benji Madden of the band Good Charlotte. Katy refuted the rumors on her blog and told her fans that for a while she would remain man-free.

Katy expressed in an interview with *Cosmopolitan* magazine that she was not the kind of person to remain single. "I don't like being single. I live this fantastic life, full of these magical things, and at the end of the day all I want to do is pick up the phone and share it with someone. The other day I'd sold a million records in the U.S. and I didn't have anyone to tell. It was actually a really lonely moment."[1]

It would not be long before she encountered Russell Brand. The two first met on the set of Brand's movie *Get Him to the Greek*.

The two shared a kissing scene, although the kiss was not to be seen by the public because it was cut entirely from the movie. Katy was giddy after that moment with Brand, even though it was only a matter of five minutes.

The two met again in September 2009 at the MTV Video Music Awards at Radio City Music Hall in New York. Brand was the host of the show and Katy was a nominee for Best Female Video for "Hot N Cold." She also sang Queen's "We Will Rock You" at the awards. Backstage, Katy and Brand bantered back and forth. Katy threw a water bottle at the actor's head during a rehearsal for the awards. This led Brand to be intrigued by Katy. He had complimented Katy on one of her bracelets at the awards' night presentation. Katy then gave the bracelet to Brand and he kept it in his pocket for the rest of the awards presentation.

Russell Brand was born June 4, 1975, in Grays, England, and had a rough childhood. His mother was battling cancer as he was growing up and his father walked out on them. His father would come in and out of his life. At the age of seven, Brand was abused by a tutor. He had a lonely childhood and he used his depression and childhood as material for his later standup act. At the age of 14, he was being bullied at school for being fat. He became a cutter and a bulimic as a teenager. This was also the time that Brand became a vegetarian. When he was aged 17, his father took him to the Far East and got him prostitutes. He was kicked out of a boarding house when a girl was found under his bed. He developed a love for acting in high school when he played Fat Sam in the school production of *Bugsy Malone*. When Brand was 16 he got into the Italia Conte stage school where he was introduced to drugs. After being expelled from the school, he enrolled at the Drama Centre, an acting academy in London. He was also expelled from this school.

It was in 1996 that Brand began doing standup comedy. He teamed up with Karl Theobald for an act they titled Theobald and Brand On Ice. Not making enough money as a comedian, he signed up for housing and disability benefits, which he received for many years. His true passion was to make people laugh. He uses his own life experiences in his act. "I've become articulate because I always felt misunderstood. I'm still littered with reminders of my anxious childhood. I was a miserable little weirdo for ages. I'm still weird."[2]

Brand continued his standup routine, continued to do drugs, and continued his womanizing. He placed fourth in the Hackney Empire's New Act of the Year competition. At the competition he found an agent named Nigel Klarfeld. He continued performing at the 2000 Edinburgh Fringe Festival with fellow comedians Mark Felgate and Shappi Khorsandi. Brand was hired by MTV as a VJ. He was fired on September 12, 2001, a day after the September 11 terrorist attacks on the United States, when he thought it was funny to come to work dressed as Osama bin Laden. From there Brand had his own TV series called *Re: Brand*. It was a documentary/comedy drama on a British cable channel.

In 2007 Brand started appearing as a host and presenter at award shows. He was a presenter at the 2007 BRIT Awards. He also participated in the *Comic Relief* and *Live Earth* at Wembley Stadium in London. He also did the *Royal Variety Performance* in 2007. He was invited to present an award at the 2008 MTV Video Music Awards and in 2009 he was asked to host the MTV Video Music Awards.

Brand is also a soccer fan. He is a huge supporter of the soccer team West Ham United and roots for this team whenever he can. He wanted to be a part of the club, but knew because of time constraints and his present career, that he could not fill the positions of player or manager. Brand decided to make a commitment to the team by serving on its board.

During this time, Brand's film acting career was also improving in the United States. By the end of 2010, Brand had acted in several movies, including *Forgetting Sarah Marshall*, *Bedtime Stories*, *The Tempest*, *Arthur*, and *Get Him to the Greek*. For *Get Him to the Greek*, Brand sang and made the soundtrack for the movie. During the film, Brand had to portray himself as a drunk and be destructive. Being sober for so long, Brand found those scenes hard to portray and it made him recollect his dark past. After these particular scenes, he would go back to his trailer and meditate and do yoga. He was nominated for an MTV Movie Award for Best Comedic Performance and three Teen Choice Awards for *Get Him to the Greek*. He also starred in *Rock of Ages* with Tom Cruise. In 2011, Brand introduced his own production company, called Branded Films. Together with Nik Linnen, Brand sought to expand his acting skills to include producing and directing. The company has offices at the Warner Bros. Studios in California.

Brand took the lead part in the movie *Arthur*, about a wealthy man who falls in love despite the risk of losing his money for that love. Brand commented that he could relate to the main character of the movie because of his love for Katy. In the movie, Arthur has no direction in his life until he becomes involved with a woman. In his real life, Brand had a transformation when he met and fell in love with Katy. Brand also admired the late actor Dudley Moore, who played Arthur in the original version, and was elated when he received the main character role in the remake. The leading female actor in the film was Greta Genvig. Brand's performance in *Arthur* showed movie critics and movie goers that Brand could play a range of characters, not just a freaky sideshow addition such as he played in *Bedtime Stories* and *Forgetting Sarah Marshall*.

Despite his acting and comedic success, Brand is still known for his strange antics. Director Oliver Stone said about Brand, "He's different, unique, a sweetheart, a rogue, a bad boy, he's completely honest, and I think he lives in another dimension. But he's burning at a very high level, and you have to wonder how long he can keep it up without burning out."[3] Brand does everything in the extreme and has done since his childhood. Brand spent time healing himself at the Keystone sex addiction clinic in Pennsylvania. He gave up alcohol and drugs in 2003. Even though during his wild days he famously had a coat he called "The Cloak of Love," Katy claims not to have known anything about his womanizing or drug abuse, which is why she accepted a date with him after meeting him again at the 2009 MTV Video Music Awards.

Brand has stated in interviews that his main goal in life is to make people laugh and he believed he had to always be "on" to achieve this goal. In 2011, Brand was named Comedy Star of the Year at CinemaCon, a gathering of movie theater owners that happens annually in Atlantic City.

On Katy's first date with Brand on September 14, 2009, he gave her a black diamond necklace and a copy of his autobiography, *My Booky Wook: A Memoir of Sex, Drugs, and Stand-Up*. Less than two weeks later the couple was vacationing together in Thailand. During that week, the two explored Eastern religions, practiced meditation, and enjoyed the togetherness, tranquility, and peace. While on the trip,

Brand introduced Katy to the art of meditating. She found that meditating helped put her mind at ease and also helped her to relax. On October 1, Katy tweeted on her account that she enjoyed a magical weekend in Thailand. Vacations to both London and Paris followed for the couple. Brand said to the media that he changed when he met and married Katy. He knew then what it meant to love and truly take care of another person. He described his relationship and marriage to Katy as companionship.

Katy made a mix tape for her new boyfriend that included songs by Jeff Buckley, Ben Folds, and Tom Waits. She also included the song "(Are You) the One That I've Been Waiting For?" by Nick Cave and the Bad Seeds. The song would later become Brand and Katy's song. Katy also hired a skywriter for $15,000 to write "I Love You" in the sky by Brand's Sunset Boulevard home. She bought Brand a $200,000 trip to outer space from Richard Branson. She also sewed his nickname, "Rusty," on the back of her clothes that she wore under her costumes so during concerts she could show her love for Brand. In November 2009, the couple went to an Australian ski resort with all of Katy's family, including her parents and her siblings. Katy then brought all of her family to New York for Christmas. Katy encouraged Brand to learn how to drive in 2010 because he did not drive at all when he lived in England. Katy bought Brand driving lessons and a Range Rover as an engagement gift.

The two purchased an old Hollywood, 1920s, art deco-style house in Los Feliz in 2009 for an estimated $3.25 million. Brand and Katy sold the first home they bought together in Los Feliz a year and a half after they purchased it. They put the four-bedroom home on the market for almost $3.4 million in the spring of 2011. The 4,600-square-foot home had four-and-a-half baths and a swimming pool. Katy accessorized the house with a pink refrigerator that she bought before they purchased the home. The appliance was not included in the sale of the home. During the couple's year and a half in the home, they redid the landscaping and converted the garage into a style room. The room held 60 feet of Katy's costumes. Because of the pair's hectic work schedules, they decided to make the change. They sold the house through Teles Property with Ernnie Carswell and Christopher Puckett being the listing agents.

Katy and then-husband Russell Brand step out for the "Change Begins Within" celebration at the Metropolitan Museum of Art on December 13, 2010. (AP Photo/Evan Agostini.)

After selling their home in Los Feliz, Katy and Brand bought a compound in the Sunset Strip of Los Angeles. The compound was once home to the former chief executive of *National Lampoon*, Daniel Laikin. Laikin bought the property in 2004 for $4.5 million and it was listed in November 2010 for $7,995,000. Laikin was found guilty of manipulating *National Lampoon*'s stock price in 2010. The Brands bought the house for $6.5 million. The gated home sits on three acres and was built in 1925. The house has a sweeping staircase, stained-glass windows, and a carved fireplace mantel in the living room. The house has seven bedrooms and nine bathrooms. It also includes a bar, a study, and a media room. The house was used in the first series of the television show *The Bachelor*.

For Christmas 2009, Brand bought Katy a trip to India. They traveled to India over New Year's Eve 2009. Katy did not know that Brand was going to propose while they were on the trip to Jaipur in India. He took Katy to an Indian fort during the day and bought Katy an authentic Indian outfit. The night got more romantic when the pair took a carriage ride to a garden for dinner. They watched the New Year's Eve fireworks on the back of an elephant. Brand had the engagement ring hidden at the hotel Taj Rambagh Palace in their Mughal Garden. In traditional style, Brand proposed while on one knee. Brand had the ring made from rare India Golconda diamonds. It was designed by jewelry artist Hanut Singh and had the inscription of the couple's song, "The one that I have been waiting for," on it. Brand described Katy in an interview with *Rolling Stone* magazine. "She's a perfectly decent, lovely person, good fun and engaging, easy to be around and interesting. But meeting her changed me. With her, I don't feel like I'm fulfilling some bizarre psychological fetish."[4] Katy affectionately calls Brand Rusty Braunstein and Rusty Rockets. When they do have time to be together, Brand and Katy like to cook, garden, and hike.

On January 6, 2010, there was a public announcement made that Katy Perry and Russell Brand were engaged. As the two were very busy touring and filming movies there was not much time for being together. On the couple's first-date anniversary in September 2010, Katy paid tribute to her fiancé with pictures of him manicured on her fingernails. Because of the release of her new album, *Teenage Dream*, Katy was very busy and had put her wedding plans on hold until the album came out. Brand, however, took the reins and bought several bride magazines to plan their wedding. "He's a total bridezilla. He's like a freak, man. You should see—he's always, like, buying bride magazines. Every time we go out for breakfast he's like, 'Can we just stop and get a bride magazine?' "[5]

Brand and Katy complement each other as a couple but they both have their flaws. They both have strong personalities and have to be the center of attention. Katy was on the lookout for someone that was stronger than she was, someone who could help her when she was down. She found Brand. When she threw the water bottle at him at the Video Music Awards, her intention was to get his attention. Katy said, "A week later we went on vacation in Thailand. I'm like, 'Oh my God, I am you. You are me.' Two divas in one house. It's like splitting an atom. It shouldn't happen."[6] Katy believes that she saved Brand from himself and his womanizing ways. Katy also knows that Brand has helped her grow as a person and has helped her gain confidence in her abilities and in her personality. Before Katy was even married to Brand, she realized that once she tied the knot it would be a balancing act.

She had to spread herself thin between her husband, her music, her family, her fans, and herself.

Friend and fellow singer Rihanna planned Katy's bachelorette party. A stretch Hummer took Katy, Rihanna, and 25 guests to the Hard Rock Café Beach Club pool. After lounging by the pool eating and drinking, the entourage went to a performance of Cirque du Soleil in Las Vegas. After that the group went to several night clubs, including Sapphire and XS. Because of her own musical career and tour dates, Rihanna could not attend the wedding. "I was upset she couldn't make it but let me promise you, there was no one more upset about it than her. When you have an album coming out you don't have a spare second in the day and you're answerable to the record company. She felt really bad she couldn't be there but we're still the very best of friends. My girl organized the best bachelorette party ever and I'll always love her to bits."[7] Katy missed Rihanna's birthday party in February 2011 because she was on her *California Dreams* tour in Portugal.

Brand and Katy made it official and wed in Rajasthan, India, on October 23, 2010. Katy paid for her family to attend the wedding and her older sister Angela was her maid of honor. Only family and friends were invited to the event. There were approximately 70 guests. The wedding took place at Aman-i-Khas Hotel, located in the Northern India countryside. It is a resort close to Ranthambore National Park, which is a wildlife sanctuary with tigers. Katy wore an Elie Saab haute couture gown. The spiritual ceremony was performed by a Christian minister, a friend of the Hudson family. During the ceremony, the two exchanged matching diamond-encrusted wedding bands. There was a rumor that Brand gave Katy a Bengal tiger named Machli for a wedding gift and Katy gave Brand a baby elephant. However, these reports are false, because tigers are a sacred animal in India and cannot be bought or sold. It was reported that animals were involved in the ceremony, as Brand was believed to make his entrance on an elephant and a tiger did nearly crash the couple's reception. After the festivities, the couple flew to the Maldives for their honeymoon. The wedding pictures have never been released in the press, although the Brands were offered a lot of money for their publication. In an interview with *Vanity Fair*, Katy explained the reason for not releasing the photographs, saying that the "press is not your friend when it comes to marriage."[8] This was especially true when rumors were flying about the couple's nuptials. When Brand and Katy heard about the rumors that were circulating about their wedding, they laughed about it. Many of the rumors were so outlandish, it was obvious that they were false. The Brands made their first public appearance as a married couple at the Europe Music Awards, where they addressed some of the rumors.

It was reported by the press that Katy and Brand had spent a week performing traditional Indian customs for their wedding which proved to be untrue as the couple arrived on the Wednesday before their wedding and left the following Monday for their honeymoon. It was also speculated that Katy kept with Indian tradition as she was allegedly wearing a nose ring with a chain to her ear. This is a traditional Indian custom that symbolizes purity and it is not to be removed until after the festivities. It is customarily removed by the groom. Later reports confirmed this was not true and Katy accessorized only with sunglasses.

The reception was held at the same hotel as the wedding. It was a loud party and the hotel has been charged with disturbing the peace during the event. There are ordinances that strictly prohibit the use of loud music after 10 p.m., a law that was not adhered to during the reception. Penalties for disobeying the ordinance range from a fine to jail time if the hotel is deemed to have done anything wrong.

When the pair went to India to get married, the paparazzi also went to India to get pictures of the couple. Outside a tiger sanctuary, Brand's bodyguards allegedly assaulted four news photographers who were trying to get pictures of Brand. The photographers were from the news services of Associated Press, Reuters, and Agence France-Presse and one from the Hindustan Times. One of the bodyguards went up to the car of one of the photographers, took the car keys, and punched the photographers. The four photographers were then stranded.

To congratulate the newlyweds, Animal Rahat and PETA of India gave Brand a bull named Russell. Poorva Joshipura, of Animal Rahat, said that both the Russells are handsome fellows. In an interview with *Reuters*, Joshipura commented, "The gift of a namesake is also fitting because just as Russell Brand embarks on his new life as a married man, Russell the bullock has also been given a new lease on life—the heavy loads he once pulled have been lifted from his shoulders for good."[9] The gift of an animal is a traditional gift in India. They gave Brand the animal because he has always been an animal rights supporter. Animal Rahat is an organization that gives free aid to animals.

As celebrities, Katy and Brand have to fend off the press while having a semi-private personal life. Both Katy and Brand have careers that involve shocking the public and gaining the public's attention in any way they know how. Brand believes the two make it happen by knowing that everything in their professional lives is pretend. Katy and Brand both know they are not perfect people and they both have a wild side. They are both at different places in their lives but they also know that they complement each other in their strengths and weaknesses.

There has also been talk about the couple having children. Katy believes it is important to enjoy each other's company before bringing babies into the relationship. Brand has said he wants a lot of children because he grew up as an only child. Katy's mother has also expressed her enthusiasm for potential grandchildren. On the red carpet at the 53rd annual Grammy Awards, Katy's mother expressed that she was ready to be a grandmother. Hudson touted her daughter's marriage to Brand, but expressed concerns as to how the two stick together with their busy schedules. Katy is focused on her career at the moment. "My singing is really important to me, but when children come along they'll be my main focus. I'd never put my career in front of my babies—it'd be a case of fitting jobs around them."[10]

The Brands have not been immune to the tabloid press. There have been rumors the couple was having marital problems and that Russell has been seen in the company of another brunette that was not Katy. The story of the couple's supposed marital strife was in the British paper *The Daily Mail* and the magazine *Heat*. *Heat* reported that Katy and Russell were close to a trial separation because they rarely saw each other due to their hectic work schedules. The tabloid stated that they had only seen each other for four days in the previous six months. This is not the first time the tabloids have been incorrect when it comes to Russell and Katy. In the spring of 2011, the Australian tabloid, *NW*, had falsely reported that Katy had cheated on Russell, after only nine months of marriage. The article, titled "World Exclusive: Katy's Other Man—Split Fears After Shock Revelation," speculated that Katy was having an affair with record producer Benny Blanco while they were working on Katy's second album. The tabloid confirmed the report with Angela Summers and Marlon David, two people Katy had never heard of. Katy responded by having her legal team address the situation. The newspaper refused to issue an apology or a retraction of the untruths so Katy took *NW* to Australia's Victoria Supreme Court. She sued for damages and aggravated damages. In a statement, Katy explained that she had been "gravely injured in her reputation and feeling [and] has suffered distress, embarrassment and humiliation."[11]

Amid rumors that Brand and Katy were having problems in their marriage, the couple retorted that they wanted to keep a low profile because they wanted to maintain some level of privacy in their personal lives. Katy used Twitter to let her fans know that there was nothing amiss in the celebrity marriage. She also criticized the tabloids for their frequent printing of misinformation.

Katy had expressed concern over actress Helen Mirren and Brand being in the movies *The Tempest* and *Arthur* together. Katy did an interview with Ellen DeGeneres on her talk show and said that she would be taking Brand's last name eventually. She also said that she was jealous of Mirren and Brand working so closely together but was glad that there was someone to take Brand off her hands for a while because the comedic actor can be a handful at times.

The couple lives in California but also maintains a two-bedroom condo in Tribeca, New York. They have the house in California because it is too cold in the winter in New York. They have three cats. Katy had one cat, Kitty Purry. Brand had one cat, Morrissey. The two bought another cat together and named it Krusty. The name is derived from Katy's name and "Rusty," the nickname Katy calls Brand. When Katy is homesick Brand sends her a text picture of their cat Krusty.

Katy learned inner beauty and confidence from Brand. They both have tattoos on their inner arms with a Sanskirt inscription that means "go with the flow." Brand is a vegetarian and a follower of the Bhakti Yoga teacher Radhanath Swami. Brand has been a vegetarian for 22 years and was named "Sexiest Vegetarian of the Year" by the organization PETA. Katy has tried to convert to her husband's eating habits but she enjoys meat too much. They both share a sense of humor and know they can be brutally honest in their relationship with each other. Brand does attend AA or NA meetings a couple of times a week and gives Katy credit for settling him down. In an interview with *Cosmopolitan* magazine, Katy said, "Everyone asks, 'How did you tame him?' It's not about taming; it's about timing. He was ready for it and so was I."[12]

With their busy lives in the entertainment industry, Katy and Brand did not have a lot of time to spend together. Many times they were seen on different parts of the world promoting their albums and movies without each other. This distance took a toll on the couple. In December 2011, the two announced that they were splitting up.

NOTES

1. Jo Berry, *Katy Perry California Gurl* (London: Orion Publishing Group, 2011), p. 85.

2. David Stone, *Russell Brand and Katy Perry: The Love Story* (London: John Blake Publishing, 2010), p. 46.

3. Erik Hedegaard, "Sexy Beast," *Rolling Stone Magazine*, June 12, 2010, p. 62.

4. Erik Hedegaard, "Sexy Beast," p. 89.

5. Jocelyn Vena, "Katy Perry Calls Fiancé Russell Brand a 'Bridezilla'," *MTV News*, March 29, 2010. www.mtvnews.com.

6. Jocelyn Vena, "Katy Perry Says She's Tamed 'Professional Prostitute' Russell Brand," *MTV News*, July 6, 2010. www.mtvnews .com.

7. Internet Movie Database. www.imdb.com.

8. Lisa Robinson, "Katy Perry's Grand Tour," *Vanity Fair*, June 2011, p. 168.

9. Brandi Fowler, "Katy Perry and Russell Brand: The Weirdest Wedding Gift Ever?!" *Entertainment Online*, October 30, 2010. www .eonline.com.

10. Internet Movie Database, www.imdb.com.

11. Gina Serpe, "Russell Brand and Katy Perry Headed to Splitsville?! Couple Hit Back at 'Trash' Tabloids,"*Entertainment Online*, July 18, 2011. www.eonline.com.

12. Alison Prato, "Katy Perry: Head Over Heels," *Cosmopolitan*, November 2010, p. 38.

Chapter 6

THE ACTRESS

Many celebrities turn to acting in their early career and throughout their careers to gain exposure and to help themselves monetarily. Katy ventured down the acting path in television and films, and has also appeared on the cover of many magazines.

Katy first appeared and modeled for Too Faced Cosmetics in 2007. At this time she was struggling to find a company who would record her songs and produce her albums, so not only did this give Katy public exposure but also helped her pay the bills. She also made a commercial for Proactive Solution acne skin medication. She believed by taking this job she would appear as a normal person with the same problems as many of her teenage fans. Fellow celebrities Jessica Simpson and Jennifer Love Hewitt have also done commercials for Proactiv.

On the March 10, 2008, episode of *Wildfire*, Katy was given a cameo as herself. In the episode, titled "Life's Too Short," she appeared as a club singer and sang one of her own songs. She also played herself in the soap opera *The Young and the Restless*. The episode, which aired June 12, 2008, had Katy appearing for a photo shoot at the magazine *Restless Style*. The plot of this particular episode was that investors may not like seeing a pop star on the cover of their magazine and this caused the controversy for the show.

When Katy's songs became popular in 2008 and 2009, she also became a sought-after musician on many of the talent shows that aired around the world. On a May 2009, *American Idol* show, she performed "Waking Up in Vegas." This led to other appearances on popular talent shows. In August 2009, she was a guest judge on the show *American Idol*, based in Los Angeles. Katy took her job on *American Idol* seriously as she toggled between being both critical and sympathetic. Having been turned down herself in her beginning years in the music industry, Katy was honest with the contestants, sometimes saying things that they didn't want to hear but that might be helpful to them. She also commented to fellow judge DioGuardi that a singer's tough and heart-felt back story does not necessarily mean they have a great singing voice and should perform on *American Idol* or receive a music contract. In many of the acts, Katy and DioGuardi did not see eye to eye. Although the onscreen tension between the two could be felt, both judges state that it was just an act and they have known each other for a long time and have no tension in their personal relationship. Katy equated the experience to a high school talent show and she is not envious of the job Simon Cowell, Kara DioGuardi, Randy Jackson, and Ellen DeGeneres had to do on a weekly basis. She was also asked to be a guest judge on *The X Factor* with Louis Walsh, Cheryl Cole, and Simon Cowell while judge Dannii Minogue was pregnant. In 2011, Dannii Minogue decided she would not return for another season of *The X Factor* because it would interfere with her obligations on another talent show, *Australia's Got Talent*. Walsh expressed interest in having both Katy and Sharon Osbourne fill the vacant seats on the show. However, neither was the final choice. N Dubz star Tulisa Contostavlos replaced Minogue. When Katy performed on *The X Factor* she performed live and wowed the crowd. Katy has said she wants to return to *The X Factor* because it is one of Brand's favorite shows. She was also asked to return as a guest judge on *American Idol* in January 2010.

In 2009 Katy was asked to make a cameo appearance in the Russell Brand film *Get Him to the Greek*. This was one of the first times she had ever met Russell Brand. In the scene, Katy and Brand kissed.

At the Nickelodeon's Kids' Choice Awards on March 27, 2010, Katy received a special gift full of slime. (AP Photo/Matt Sayles.)

The scene was later left on the cutting room floor. According to Brand, Katy was not a believable actress in Get Him to the Greek and that is why the scene is not in the movie. In an interview with Ryan Seacrest, Brand explained, "We cut it out because her acting was so atrocious it ruined the film. It just made the film boring and rubbish."[1] Known for joking all the time, Brand's remarks were seen as retaliation for Katy's earlier comments that compared Brand to Jim Morrison, Dudley Moore, Oscar Wilde, Charles Manson, and Elvis Presley. Brand claims there was chemistry even with their first movie kiss.

Katy was asked to present the Favorite Movie Actress Award at the Nickelodeon Kids' Choice Awards. The awards took place at the UCLA Campus in Los Angeles, on March 27, 2010. As at all Nickelodeon Awards, someone is always slimed for the entertainment of the audience. Katy was slimed when she opened the box to reveal Miley Cyrus as the winner of the award.

Katy was asked to be on the popular children's show Sesame Street. She was to perform a rendition of her single "Hot N Cold" with Elmo the puppet to teach children about opposites. Katy was wearing a low-cut dress and singing with Elmo. After the segment had aired on

YouTube many parents expressed their disapproval of the piece. They complained that too much of Katy's chest was present for a children's show. The episode would not be aired on the television program. In an ironic twist, Elmo appeared on the talk show *Good Morning America* saying he was disappointed that the snippet was not aired.

Katy also made a guest appearance on the television show *How I Met Your Mother*. She played Honey, Zoey's ditzy cousin. She caught the eye of womanizer Barney, who impressed Honey by telling her he had four Nobel prizes. Katy likes Neil Patrick Harris and enjoyed the cast and appreciated their patience with her bad acting skills.

Shortly after the *Sesame Street* fiasco, Katy appeared on the September 27, 2010, episode of *Saturday Night Live*. She sang two songs, "California Gurls" and "Teenage Dream." She also appeared in the skit Bronx Beat where she took the opportunity to poke fun at the Elmo skit with a skit of her own. She came out wearing a shirt with a picture of Elmo on it that was torn to reveal her cleavage.

Katy's performing with animated characters did not stop at *Sesame Street*. In 2010 she also landed the voiceover role as Smurfette in the film *The Smurfs*. *The Smurfs* cartoon originated in Belgium. Some believe that Smurfette was added to the cartoon to show that the male Smurfs were heterosexual. Other interpretations are that Smurfette was added to the series to appeal to girls. Smurfette, throughout the years, has been the most merchandised character. Smurfette was made by the evil sorcerer Gargamel out of clay to bring the Smurf village down. However, the Smurfs were so sweet to Smurfette that she decided she wanted to be a real Smurf. Papa Smurf made a potion to turn her into a real Smurf. Growing up, Katy was not allowed to watch *The Smurfs* because of the sorcery. She accepted the part willingly, though, as she said, "It makes sense to me because I feel like I am a cartoon! So it's a natural progression to do animation."[2] The real-life actors in the movie are Neil Patrick Harris and Jayma Mays. Katy played Smurfette alongside Jonathan Winters as Papa Smurf, George Lopez as Grouchy Smurf, Kevin James as Hefty Smurf, Alan Cumming as Gutsy Smurf, and Hank Azaria as Gargamel. The film was released in theaters on July 23, 2010, and opened number two at the box office. Katy had a dress made for the premiere of *The Smurfs* at the Ziegfeld Theatre in

On July 24, 2011, Katy
appears at the premiere of The
Smurfs. Katy was the voice of
Smurfette in the movie, released
in 2011. (AP Photo/Evan
Agostini, file.)

New York City. The dress was a strapless, knee-length dress that featured a sequined Smurfette on the front. Because of the success of *The Smurfs* movies, Sony Pictures immediately planned a sequel with a release date of August 2, 2013, for a film titled *The Smurfs 2*. It is not certain what the plot line will be or who the actors will be in the sequel. In two months, *The Smurfs* film grossed more than $135 million. Katy enjoyed working on the animated film partly because she could come to work in her pajamas if she needed to.

Harris and Azaria, Katy's co-stars in *The Smurfs* movie, became friendly with Katy during the production. Harris especially took to Katy's charisma and personality. In an interview with *MTV News*, Harris commented, "Katy can do no wrong in my book. She's tall, she's funny, she can sing and has a sharp wit and is a savvy businesswoman. I say Katy Perry may take over the world. I will be her vice president."[3] Azaria first met Katy at *The Smurfs* movie premiere. Because it's an animated film, the actors and actresses can come in separately to do their voice-overs, and it is not uncommon for them not to meet each other during the film. Azaria was excited by Katy's pop-star attitude.

In Spain, *The Smurfs* movie premiered in the town of Juzcar. For the debut, the whole town was painted in blue. The residents of Juzcar were elated that they were chosen as the Smurfs village.

On August 10, 2010, Katy was a guest on the *Today Show*. Her entrance was made descending from the ceiling on a cotton candy cloud. She brought her candy-themed stage that she used for her concerts, including the lollipops and the Gummi bears. In between songs, she took the time to give autographs to her adoring fans, many of whom had camped out the night before in order to see their favorite artist in the flesh. She ended her performance by singing "I Kissed a Girl," a song she said was one of the first songs she sang on her first appearance on the *Today Show*.

On November 11, 2010, Katy performed at the Victoria's Secret Fashion Show. The show was filmed on a New York ferry. She performed "Firework" and a medley of her other hits. Together with singer Akon, Katy crooned as the models walked down the stage to show off the latest year's fashions. Katy wore some outfits during the show that looked like lingerie. For her song "Firework" she wore a purple leotard but changed her costume when she performed her other songs. She wore a yellow, heart-covered dress and high boots when she sang the songs "Teenage Dream," "Hot N Cold," and "California Gurls." True to her fashion, Katy changed outfits several times during the performances, which audiences have come to expect from her.

Katy ended 2010 by acting in *The Simpsons* episode "The Fight before Christmas." She played herself in the animated scenes and was portrayed as Moe the bartender's girlfriend. During the show she also played in live-action scenes with puppet versions of *The Simpsons*. In one of the scenes, Katy is a live person, dancing with puppets of the Simpsons and cast of characters. In the holiday special she also kisses Mr. Burns to which he replies, "I kissed a girl and I liked it." The episode aired on December 5, 2010.

Katy made a guest appearance on MTV's show *Randy Jackson Presents America's Best Dance Crew* in 2011. She was named the "Superstar of the Week." The remaining teams competing on the show then had to dance to some of Katy's hits, including "Waking Up in Vegas," "Teenage Dream," "Hot N Cold," and "Firework."

Aside from having her face in films and on television, Katy has appeared on more than 15 different magazine covers, including the June 2011 *Vanity Fair* cover. On the cover she looks like a pin-up model, with long, wavy black hair with half of her hair covering her eye. She wore a strapless, revealing dress. In the article Katy talked about everything from her strict upbringing to getting married to wild-man Brand. Katy also appeared on the cover of *Harper's* Bazaar for its holiday issue in 2010. For the spread she covered her lips in 150 red Swarovski Element crystals. The photo was taken by Alexi Lubomirski. Katy has appeared twice on the cover of *Rolling Stone* since her second album came out. She posed for the cover of *Rolling Stone* in August 2010 and for the double summer issue in 2011. Photographer Mark Seliger took the photographs. Katy recalled her childhood in the interview with the magazine, recounting that she was not allowed to say she was lucky when she was growing up. Her parents taught her to say that she was blessed.

Katy also posed scantily clad for the cover of the men's magazine, *Maxim* for the January 2011 issue. For the June/July 2009 issue of *Complex* magazine, she appears on the cover in black leggings and a black corset. The nine-photo spread of Katy depicts a darker side of the musician and is far removed from the fruit and candy-wearing girl her fans had been familiar with. In an interview for the article, Katy expressed that her first album, *One of the Boys*, was written between the ages of 17 and 23. Like her songs, she has grown into a more mature style and needs to appear more like a woman in her middle twenties.

Us Weekly magazine devoted a special issue to Katy in 2011. It featured photos taken on her 2011 *California Dreams* tour. The magazine walked readers through the sets on the tour. The article also included quotes from Katy about different subjects such as her music, her childhood, her new life with Brand, and her likes and dislikes.

Her songs have also gained fame by being used in films. In 2008 her song "Fingerprints" appeared on the soundtrack for the film *Baby Mama*. The movie *When In Rome* uses Katy's popular songs "If You Can Afford Me" and "Starstrukk." "Hot N Cold" has been a popular song in both films and on television. It can be heard in the movies *The Ugly Truth* and the *American Pie* sequel *American Pie Presents: The Book of*

Love; and it is sung by the Chipettes in *Alvin and the Chipmunks: The Squeakquel.* On television, the song was used on 90210, the new TV series, and on *Ghost Whisperer.* "Self-Inflicted" and "Thinking of You" were played on the MTV Series *The Hills.* Her single "Fingerprints" was the theme song for Oxygen Network's series *Girls.* "I Kissed a Girl" was also used in an episode of *Gossip Girls.* Katy has also lent her voice to the video game genre. She recorded a song in Simlish for the game *Sims 2: Apartment Life.* Total Sci-Fi Online conducted a poll to see which woman their fans would choose to play Wonder Woman in the film that is in its early stages. Katy won the poll with 20 percent of the vote. Other celebrities that received votes were Megan Fox, Monica Bellucci, Angelina Jolie, and Gemma Arterton. Beyoncé Knowles has expressed interest in playing the role.

For many celebrities, it is important to be a versatile musician, actor, and performer to be exposed to as many fans as possible. Katy has proven that she also has the ability to entertain in other avenues besides performing in concerts and videos.

NOTES

1. Sadao Turner, "Russell Brand: Katy Perry's 'Atrocious' Acting Led to Her Being Cut from Greek," June 4, 2010. www.ryanseacrest .com.

2. Alison Prato, "Katy Perry: Head Over Heels," *Cosmopolitan,* November 2010, p. 36.

3. Jocelyn Vena, "Katy Perry 'May Take Over the World,' *The Smurfs* Co-Stars Say." *MTV News,* July 26, 2011. www.mtvnews.com.

Chapter 7

GIVING BACK

Katy believes she must always remember where she came from to keep her humble. Like many other celebrities Katy demonstrates her philanthropy by giving to certain organizations and supporting others with her performances. The main charities Katy supports are breast cancer research and various AIDS groups.

A well-endowed woman, Katy used this attribute to help breast cancer awareness in 2008. She took a plaster cast of her chest and decorated it. She sold the piece at auction for $3500 with all the proceeds given to breast cancer awareness. For the auction, Travis McCoy, Katy's boyfriend at the time, decorated his sneakers to be donated. Other things donated to the online auction were decorated sneakers from the Vans Warped Tour. Images of artists from the Warped Tour, taken by Erin Caruso, were also available to bid on.

In 2008, Katy aided Project Clean Water, a charity formed in 1997 by Jewel to help millions of people have access to clean water and improve their quality of life. Katy donated handwritten lyrics to several of her songs for a charity Internet auction. The organization has been responsible for building wells and infiltration systems in several countries such as India, Tanzania, and Bangladesh and countries in Central America.

Every year, the Grammy Foundation puts on a charity auction to benefit MusiCares, an organization that helps those in need in the music industry. Katy donated a VIP experience with her, so the highest bidder had a meet and greet with Katy. Several other celebrities gave of their time and talent for the 2009 auction. Winners could have received a phone call with Aretha Franklin or a day on the set of a Rihanna music video or photo shoot. Other musicians signed memorabilia to be auctioned off, including books, CDs, guitars, and drums. Some of the familiar names included Katy, Taylor Swift, Christina Aguilera, and Jesse McCarthy.

In February of 2009, Katy participated in an auction for the Habitat for Humanity of the Greater Los Angeles area. The online auction was at the site Clothes Off Our Back and had hardhats signed by celebrity volunteers and supporters of the cause. The hardhats were designed and signed by music, television, and film stars. Some of the music stars that helped, besides Katy, were Green Day, Justin Timberlake, Miley Cyrus, Taylor Swift, and Vanessa Hudgens. Also in 2009, Katy participated in the T-Mobile MyFaves Shot of a Lifetime in Phoenix. Katy offered her voice to entertain the crowd after the main event of trying to shoot hoops for $50,000 was over.

On May 16, 2009, Katy attended the Life Ball in Austria. The event raises funds for HIV/AIDS charities that help projects all around the world. Katy headlined the show. The money raised helped men, women, and children in impoverished countries who are affected by AIDS but do not have medicine or doctors to treat the disease. The ball is the only AIDS charity ball that has ever taken place in a government building and it raised millions of dollars.

The television game show *Who Wants to Be a Millionaire* held a charity series where celebrities could win up to $50,000 for the charity of their choice. They received four life lines, including phone a friend, ask the audience, double dip, and ask an expert, who during Katy's performance was reporter and news anchor, Sam Donaldson. Katy chose St. Jude's Children's fund as the charity she played for. The question presented was, "What young celebrity has the Italian phrase 'Live without regrets' tattooed on her back with regrets spelled incorrectly?"

Before Katy heard the question she asked if she could phone a friend. To the delight of the audience, Regis Philbin commented that Katy had to hear the question before she could use the phone a friend life line. She used her phone a friend life line to call Shannon Woodward, one of her closest friends. Katy's options for the answer to the question were Hilary Duff, Hayden Panettiere, Vanessa Hudgens, or Kristen Bell. Between Katy and her friend, the two answered Hayden Panettiere, the correct answer. Katy won $50,000 for her charity. Other musical guests included Snoop Dogg.

In 2009, Katy joined with Cyndi Lauper, Yoko Ono, and the band N.E.R.D. to design shirts for AIDS awareness. The celebrities participated in the second annual Fashion Against AIDS. Each T-shirt was designed with a message about AIDS awareness. Katy's bodysuit and T-shirts were emblazoned with the message "WHAT'S ON THE OUTSIDE IS WHAT COUNTS." The clothing was sold at H&M clothing stores, which have 1,500 stores in 28 different countries. The 2010 celebrity participants included Timbaland, Rihanna, and Ziggy Marley.

Katy began her musical writing career when she was given a guitar at the age of 13. In an effort not to forget where she came from, she autographed a guitar for the Miami GuitarTown project in 2009. She signed the guitar when she was in Fort Lauderdale for a concert on her *Hello Katy* tour. The guitar was an Epiphone and was painted and decorated by visual artist Jonathan Stein. The Miami GuitarTown project is a public art display of decorated Gibson and Epiphone guitars. The sculptures were spread all over Miami and auctioned off in the fall to local charities. The event was sponsored by the Gibson Foundation.

On September 14, 2010, Katy went back to her high school, Don Pueblos High School. She held a performance for 2,000 students at the school. During her performance she dedicated a song to Shane Lopes, a boy she had a crush on when she attended the school.

Together with Russell Brand, she attended the Noreen Fraser Foundation benefit, called "Variety's Power of Comedy," sponsored by Bing and The Sims. The event was held to raise money to support women's cancer research. Brand was honored during the presentation. He told the audience that his mother had had cancer three times during her lifetime.

Katy, along with Pink, donated a pair of her shoes for people injured by landmines. She gave a pair of her brown suede Report Signature heels to the auction. The shoes in the auction were signed by the celebrity who owned them. The eBay auction, titled "MAGS Give Landmines the Boot," went from July 22 to August 1, 2010. All the money raised from the event goes to clearing landmines all around the world.

For Breast Cancer Awareness Month in October 2010, Katy helped Stand Up for Cancer. She donated memorabilia for an online celebrity charity auction. The event was held in conjunction with public service announcements, a way to donate to breast cancer awareness through texting, and a 10K/5K run. The radio station envisioned including the musicians they play and their listeners to bring breast cancer awareness to the public.

Also in 2010 Katy used her Web site to encourage fans to make a video on YouTube of someone that was inspirational. The winner, Georgia student Cory Woodard, was chosen in January 2011. He believed his mother was an inspirational figure because she had always supported and cared for him and he was wheelchair-bound. Woodard was awarded a trip to London with three of his friends for a Katy Perry concert.

In December 2010, Katy participated in a performance to honor military service members called "USO Presents: VH1 Divas Salute to the Troops." The event was sponsored by music television station VH1 and took place at the Marine Corps Station Miramar located in San Diego, California. Kathy Griffin hosted the presentation. The show included performers, presenters, special guests, and commentary from troops on the front lines. Divas.VH1.com also had a Web link with news and information about the show. A photo mosaic was created so people could add their photos to show their support for the troops. VH1 donated $1, up to $10,000, for each photo shared, to USO's Operation Ending Care. As "diva" refers to those female performers who have taken the spotlight, supporters tune in to see the present cast of divas for the year. Other "divas" that sang at the USO event were Adele, Kelly Clarkson, Miley Cyrus, and Leona Lewis. For the concert, Katy performed Cyndi Lauper's hit "Girls Just Wanna Have Fun" and her own song, "Firework."

Katy featured a contest on her Web site before the "Firework" video was produced. She was looking for 250 extras to perform in the video. She wanted people to nominate those that had been a "firework" and made a difference in the lives of others. The video was dedicated to the Gets Better Project, which encourages the fight against discrimination.

Katy participated in the Z100 Jingle Ball Concert at Madison Square Garden in New York on December 10, 2010. For 2010, the ball benefitted Musicians On Call, an organization that was formed in 1999. The charity brings live and recorded music to patients in healthcare facilities to help with the healing process. The charity benefits patients, families, and caregivers. For every ticket sold to the Jingle Ball concert, $1 was donated to Musicians On Call. Other famous people that performed at the ball included Justin Bieber, Bruno Mars, Michael Bublé, Selena Gomez, and others.

December was a big month for Katy in 2010 when it came to giving to charities and performing at fundraisers. On December 22, 2010, Katy sang on the CBS television special, *The 12th Annual A Home for Christmas*. The event is put on annually to show people the joys of adoption. The special is sponsored by the Dave Thomas Foundation for Adoption and the Children's Action Network. More than 20,000 foster children have been adopted because of this holiday special. Other musical guests included Maroon 5, Ricky Martin, and Melissa Etheridge. Also in 2010, Katy sang with *Glee* actor Darren Criss at the Trevor Live Benefit for the Trevor Project. The project is an awareness campaign to provide suicide and crisis intervention services for gay, lesbian, and transgender people. Criss sang Katy's hit "Teenage Dream." Katy made a surprise entrance after his performance, to the delight of the crowd. The audience rose to its feet and applauded for the two celebrities. Other celebrities performing at the event included Neil Patrick Harris, Sarah Silverman, Queen Latifah, and Angelina Jolie.

Katy went political in 2010 when she supported the repeal of the military "Don't Ask, Don't Tell" policy. She tweeted her enthusiasm after fellow music star Pink posted comments. They were elated that after 17 years of the military policy, Obama and the Senate finally voted that it was unconstitutional. When New York became the sixth state to allow gay marriages, Katy, together with Lady Gaga and Pink, vocally supported the decision on Twitter. Katy commented that New York had become the coolest place on Earth. Husband Brand also tweeted "carpe diem" in response to the news. LeAnn Rimes, Pink, Lady Gaga, and Katy's co-star and actor friend Neil Patrick Harris also posted their elation over the passage of the bill.

In the spring of 2011, Katy participated in a record-breaking 51-hour *Comic Relief* special in London, England. For the show she was seen wearing a costume with a big red nose (for Red Nose Day). The event raised £2.4 million. Comic Relief is an organization based in the United Kingdom that raises funds for a just world free from poverty. They raise funds through entertainment and basically have two main fundraisers, Red Nose Day and Sport Relief.

In an effort to help Japan after the devastation from the earthquake and tsunami, musicians got together to help the Japanese Red Cross in their efforts to help people and clean up the area. Along with other artists like Adele, Beyoncé, Madonna, Lady Gaga, Justin Bieber, and others, Katy recorded a charity album, titled *Songs for Japan*. The album was released on March 25, 2011. The album was available on iTunes for $9.99 with all proceeds going directly to the Japanese Red Cross. Thirty-eight songs were available on the compilation as well as a 2-CD set that was available for purchase. Some of the songs included Katy's "Firework," John Lennon's "Imagine," Lady Gaga's "Born This Way," and Justin Bieber's "Pray." Even the record companies, EMI Music, Sony Music Entertainment, Universal Music Group, and Warner Music Group forewent royalties so more money would go to the Red Cross. By the middle of 2011, $5 million had been raised to help the victims in Japan, which equates to more than 500,000 copies of the collaboration sold. After the devastation in Japan from the earthquake and tsunami, followed by a nuclear crisis and mass evacuations of the country, Katy took to Twitter to encourage her fans to pray and donate to the people of Japan. Other celebrities joined Katy in her efforts to raise money through Twitter, including P. Diddy, Conan O'Brien, and Chris Brown.

Katy also stepped up to help those in Australia devastated by the floods there. While on her *California Dreams* tour she encouraged everyone to give for the relief of those affected by the Australian floods.

Katy has special light wands that fans can purchase that are waved during her song "Firework." The money raised by the purchase of the light wands benefitted the Red Cross for Queensland Flood Relief. From the sale of the wands, Katy has raised more than $35,000 for both Japan and Australia.

Together with Ubisoft, a video game manufacturer in the United Kingdom, Katy sponsored a contest called "Just Dance Your Way to Katy Perry." In the United Kingdom, Katy's songs and style have been compared to that of singer Avril Lavigne. Contestants had to record themselves and friends dancing to Katy's "Firework" song. Winners received tickets to the concert in the United Kingdom and a meet and greet with Katy backstage after the show. Those who attended Katy's United Kingdom concerts were able to play Just Dance 3 and also see Katy playing the video game. Katy has lent her songs to the Just Dance series of video games before. "Hot N Cold" was available on the first Just Dance video game with "Firework" being available on both the second and third versions of Just Dance. The Just Dance game is available on Wii, Xbox 360, and PlayStation 3.

Katy raised money for her idol Freddie Mercury's charity by dressing up as Freddie in 2011. She donned a cropped wig, a moustache, and a bright yellow jacket in a tribute to the Queen star. The Freddie For a Day campaign raised awareness for the Mercury Phoenix Trust, an AIDS charity. Mercury died from AIDS-related pneumonia in 1991. Katy designed a T-shirt for the H&M store with all the proceeds going to AIDS research.

In September 2011, Katy joined with other artists, such as Foo Fighters, to pay tribute to Freddie Mercury, Queen's lead singer, who would have celebrated his 65th birthday in 2011. They recorded special video messages that included thanking the music icon for his contribution to music and his influence on many artists. Katy thanked him for being such an influence on her recording career and for encouraging her to enter the music industry.

Katy used ticket sales from her *California Dreams* tour to help charity. For the North American portion of the tour, those who purchased tickets at Tickets-for-Charity were able to direct a portion of the proceeds to a charity of their choice through an option that was available at checkout. Among the charities selected were the Humane Society of the United States and the Children's Health Fund. More than $150,000 was raised to help charities in North America.

Together with Brand, Katy plans to start a charity of her own that will help the homeless and the poor. She believes that since she is so successful, some of her money should be used to help others in need. In an interview with *Grazia,* a British magazine, Katy explained, "Russell has changed his life and wants to help other people change theirs. For all his naughtiness on the surface, underneath, he's truly good. My parents adore him. People laugh when I say Russell is a man of God but I'm just waiting for them to see what he does. We have this plan to set up a foundation to help people, feed them, clothe them, give shelter. We don't want to use our fame just to sit on our money on a mountain, we want to do something with it."[1]

NOTE

1. "Katy Perry and Russell Brand Want to Start a Charity," *Teen Music,* December 25, 2010. www.teenmusic.com.

Chapter 8

CONTROVERSY

Everyone opens themselves up to scrutiny and criticism when they decide they want to pursue a career in front of the public. Katy has had her share of controversy from everything from her song lyrics, to her dresses, to her name itself.

With songs titled "I Kissed a Girl," "Ur so Gay," and "Waking Up in Vegas," there was bound to be some backlash from some organizations and even other musicians. Many parents believe that Katy's songs promote underage drinking, have sexual undertones, and are not appropriate for children and teenagers.

When "I Kissed a Girl" came out in the summer of 2008, it stayed on the Billboard Hot 100 for seven weeks and sold more than 3.1 million downloads. Despite its popularity, the song was not a hit with everyone. Katy's mother expressed her distaste for the song in an interview with *The Daily Mail*. She said, "I hate the song. It clearly promotes homosexuality and its message is shameful and disgusting. Katy knows how I feel. I can't even listen to that song. The first time I heard it I was in total shock. When it comes on the radio, I bow my head and pray."[1] Katy's mother continued to preach about how as parents they must love their daughter because she is a child of God. They do love her but know that they do not have to agree with everything that she says, just as Katy does not have to believe everything that her parents believe in. They have cited the Bible as judging homosexuality as a sin, but that the Bible also teaches forgiveness, so they focus on that aspect when it comes to their daughter's lyrics.

Despite the disapproval that Hudson expressed in the press about the "I Kissed a Girl" lyrics, Katy said that her parents are still very supportive. They enjoyed Katy's other songs on the *One of the Boys* album. Katy's parents vocalized their concerns and distaste for the songs "I Kissed a Girl" and "Ur So Gay," but Katy knows that they were singing along with her other fans to songs like "Waking Up in Vegas."

Pastor David Allison of the Havens Corner Church in Blacklick, Ohio, went so far as to go on *NBC News* in 2008 to express his opinion that he believed the song promoted homosexuality. He also thought the song encouraged teenagers to experiment with homosexuality. He went on to remind people that homosexuality is not condoned in the Bible. The marquee in front of his Ohio church read, "I kissed a girl and liked it, then I went to Hell." The organization Focus on the Family also came out strongly against the song.

Some radio stations refused to play the song. It was rumored that in Singapore the song was banned altogether. Some stores even refused to sell the album. Three Texas high school cheerleaders were suspended for using the song in a routine during football games. Mario Barros, a teacher in Brazil, had used the song "I Kissed a Girl" in his curriculum. He was fired from his teaching position because the headmaster believed the song promoted alcohol and sexuality.

Gay and lesbian groups attacked "I Kissed a Girl," as well as the song "Ur So Gay," because they saw the lyrics as Katy poking fun at their lifestyle. The groups were upset because she was exploiting gay and lesbian communities to sell records. They believed that Katy's lyrics were saying that their behavior was wrong or immoral.

Even fellow musicians were making negative comments about the song. Jill Sobule had written a song titled "I Kissed a Girl" in 1995 and was upset because she believed Katy got the song title from her. Katy had told followers and the media that the lyrics and the title came to her in a dream. Both musicians were signed by the same executive at Capitol Records but at different times. You cannot copyright a song title, so Katy was well within her right to use the words. Beth Ditto, who plays with the band Gossip, said Katy's lyrics were offensive to gay culture. A well-known gay activist, Ditto claimed that to Katy the song is just a party song to sell records and to get onto the music charts. She was quoted as saying, "I don't care if she writes about kissing a girl, but there are people who kiss girls in their everyday life, and it's not as easy as just kissing a girl and everyone loving you."[2]

Katy took the comments with a grain of salt and believed that a musician insulting another songwriter's work was tacky and unnecessary. Katy was interviewed by a London paper after the attack by Ditto. She said, "I heard that she (Ditto) said something about me. I don't want to get into a slanging war with anybody, so I don't want to say anything bad about her. But I am not impressed. I've learnt in the past year that one artist should never insult another artist's music—it's tacky."[3] In another interview with *Out Magazine*, Katy said that people in the United States were looking for things that offend them. She said when she travels to places like Europe, journalists do not see the sensationalism or shock value of her songs. She explained, "I get a lot of journalists in Europe who act like 'What's the big deal? People are OK with hip-hop videos where there are strippers and drugs and gangs and guns, when you're singing about an innocent kiss.' I'm aware of people's opinions, but it won't change how I express myself as an artist."[4] *Out Magazine* rated Katy as its 2008 Musician of the Year.

Katy has admitted to Katie Couric that she has kissed girls a couple of times. Even when she participated in the Warped Tour in 2008 she kissed 16-year-old Jenna Buhmann while performing the song in George, Washington. Eventually, the media lost interest until the next song "Ur So Gay" was released. Katy was quoted as saying, "Have I ever kissed a girl? Of course I have. I can't sing a song and not have done it. That'd be complete hypocrisy. I fancy Scarlett Johansson, Natalie Portman, and Angelina Jolie—I'd definitely kiss them."[5]

Although Katy's parents support her by going to her shows and even appeared in her music video for "Hot N Cold," they also use Katy, her lyrics, and her provocativeness in their ministry. Keith preaches that he thinks Satan has pulled Katy away from the fold. In a dramatic way, Keith uses Katy's lyrics in his sermons by saying, "I kissed God—and I liked it." Because of Katy's notoriety, the Hudsons are famous too and reach out to churches all around the world to preach their message. However, they may have been less successful if they weren't Katy's parents. Keith does not answer questions about his daughter but is happy to share her with his congregation. Katy used the opportunity in an interview with Katie Couric to reveal that although her parents are preaching now, they were not always like that. They used to party in the company of rock stars and pop culture icons. Katy said that what her parents did far outweigh the stories of wildness she has to tell. "My parents have stories. They probably have better stories than I do. And they found God. They needed to find God. Not that they needed to find God, but God found them, really," Katy explained as she and Couric walked backstage.[6]

There are some people who believe that the Hudsons are using their daughter Katy for their own success and financial gain. On a recent trip to London to see their daughter perform, they also preached in one of the churches in a last-minute decision. They expensed the trip as a tax-write off because they also performed their ministry work. Ray Toms, the pastor of the church where the Hudsons ministered that trip, said the Hudsons came 10 minutes before the service was to begin. "To be quite honest, one or two people in our church didn't take to them. They felt these people were cashing in on their daughter's fame. But a lot of young people turned up because of the Katy Perry connection and five of them made a fresh commitment to God that day."[7]

Ditto again commented about the lyrics in "Ur So Gay" and continued to call Katy offensive to the gay community. The song also stirred emotions in the Internet world. Zach Rosen and blogger Duane Moody expressed that they were insulted by the lyrics and posted their disgruntled views on *The New Gay* Web site. Peter Tatchell, a well-known gay activist, responded that the lyrics demean gay people. "I am sure Katy would get a critical reception if she expressed comparable sentiments in a song called UR so black, Jewish, or disabled," he responded to a London paper.[8]

In the song "Ur So Gay," Katy used her experiences with an ex-boyfriend who had some of the characteristics of gay men. She had intended the song to be a joke. Katy says the world is metrosexual. Her other song "Waking Up in Vegas" was scrutinized for promoting underage drinking and fake IDs. There were several references to sex in the song. Because of its content, the song was banned during many school dances.

Fortunately for Katy her second album *Teenage Dream* caused less controversy than her *One of the Boys* album. The album, *Teenage Dream*, was slapped with a parental advisory for explicit content. The cover of the album had Katy lying naked on a candy cloud, posing in her popular pin-up style. As this was her candy-themed album, pink cotton candy covers her bottom on the cover. The videos for the songs on Katy's album were also labeled "sexually charged."

In the spring of 2010, the single "California Gurls" was released. The song was an immediate success with iTunes selling more than a million downloads in the first four weeks. The song was recorded with Katy and musical artist Snoop Dogg. After the song's release, the Beach Boys demanded a co-credit and royalties for the song. In one part of the song Snoop Dogg sings the lyric, "I wish they all could be California girls," a line that is also in the "California Girls" song recorded by the Beach Boys in 1965. They did not sue Katy, but filed a diminutive claim over the lyrics. In a *CBS News* interview, a Beach Boys spokesperson said, "Using the words or melody in a new song taken from an original work is not appropriate under any circumstances, particularly from one as well-known and iconic as 'California Girls.'"[9]

By August 2011, China had banned songs from Lady Gaga, Katy Perry, and the Backstreet Boys. China's Ministry of Culture instructed downloadable sites to delete the songs or face some kind of punishment. Katy's "Last Friday Night (T.G.I.F.)" was among the pop songs that were banned. Lady Gaga had six songs that were banned in China, including "The Edge of Glory," "Hair," "Marry the Night," "Americano," "Judas," and "Bloody Mary." The Backstreet Boys song "I Want It That Way," released in 2001, was also listed on the newest release of songs banned in China. The American pop artists were not the only musicians hit by the ban. The list also included Hong Kong and Taiwanese songs. Songs are supposed to be submitted to China's Ministry of Culture for mandatory government screening and approval. This process is to preserve the national cultural security of the nation. The government censored songs because of political messages and commentaries that may be detrimental to China.

Katy's costumes of fruit and candy may seem quirky but they are what makes her shows entertaining and unique. Other outfits, however, have caused a stir. In 2010, Katy posed topless for the cover of *Esquire* magazine. In 2010 she was also invited to perform on *Sesame Street* with Elmo, singing about opposites to the tune of her song "Hot N Cold." The Giles Dean wedding dress outfit that she wore caused a stir because it revealed too much of her cleavage. She wore the wedding dress as a statement of her future wedding with actor Russell Brand. The dress included a veil and a piece of mesh above her chest, much like professional skaters wear with their outfits. Parents complained when the segment was shown on YouTube. They believed that her dress was inappropriate to be shown on a program that was aimed at preschool-aged children. *Sesame Street* executives were quick to release a statement in favor of parents, explaining that they value parents' opinions. Makers of *Sesame Street* did not want to upset parents because their research has shown that children learn better when watching programs with a parent or guardian. The segments on *Sesame Street* are geared toward both adults and children. Many comments weren't necessarily disrespecting the skit, but rather were offended that Katy was even on *Sesame Street*. With the shock value Katy sometimes has in her lyrics and dress, some parents think she should have never been chosen to appear on *Sesame Street*. Despite all the negative feedback, there were some that saw no harm in the video at all. The comments stated that the skit was cute and were even disappointed it was taken off YouTube because kids enjoyed it. The segment never aired on the television show. Katy retaliated several weeks later when she guest-starred on the comedy show *Saturday Night Live*. One skit had her wearing a tight Elmo shirt that was purposely cut to show her cleavage and expose what all the fuss was about.

Katy's parents have noticed the way their daughter dresses and do not always approve of her choices. In an article in the *New York Post*, Katy's mom is quoted as saying, "No mom wants to see the top of her daughter's boobs."[10] Being evangelical ministers, Katy's parents have a more conservative way of thinking and dressing. "Some (of her clothes) are too revealing and her father has had words with her about it. Like any child she is going through a period of rebellion."[11]

Despite the continued controversy about her lyrics and costumes, Katy has shown that her style is what sells albums. Both her albums, *One of the Boys* and *Teenage Dream*, have reached platinum status.

Her concerts are performed all over the world to sold-out audiences. With her growing popularity, she has placed herself in the middle of the press hoopla where her comments and behavior could be misconstrued.

In 2008, Katy made a comment that was taken out of context. She had described herself as a "fatter version of Amy Winehouse and the skinnier version of Lily Allen."[12] Allen, a singer and fashion designer, took offense to what Katy said. Katy apologized but it was too late. Allen blasted Katy back on the London station Capital FM. Allen's grudge with Katy went further than just her comment in the press. She believed Katy was being marketed as the American version of her. In an interview with *MTV News*, she said, "I didn't say anything that was rude, I just said she wasn't English and she doesn't write her own songs."[13] Allen also threatened to take the feud to Facebook if Katy had anything to say in retaliation and threatened to put Katy's phone number on Facebook. She ended the interview by telling *MTV News* that there is really nothing negative between she and Katy Perry and the issue has been resolved.

Katy has also had a few run-ins with fellow quirky musician Lady Gaga. The two have similar styles in that their outfits are intended to entertain and shock audiences. In an interview published in the *Daily Mirror*, it was reported that Katy said that Lady Gaga looked like she had male genitalia and she just dresses like a man and a woman to get press. Katy said that she was on a flight from Australia when the interview supposedly took place and could not have said those things anyway. In another unrelated incident, Lady Gaga had told her fans that her alter ego, Yuyi, a mermaid, may appear in her next music video. Katy posted a picture of herself dressed as a mermaid on her Twitter account. Fans of both Lady Gaga and Katy posted that Katy only took the picture after the announcement that Lady Gaga would be Yuyi the mermaid in her next video after Lady Gaga wore a mermaid costume in her video for "The Edge of Glory." Although the singers bantered back and forth as to who came up with the mermaid persona first, pop singer Madonna actually posed as a mermaid first in her 1989 music video for "Cherish." Madonna has been a musical icon for more than 30 years and has been imitated by many female singers, including Lady Gaga and Katy.

Katy uses Twitter to communicate her feelings to her fans when she feels she has been wronged or when she is elated about something. She took to Twitter to defend herself against comments that were misconstrued about artists using product placements in their videos. Product placing means using brand-specific products, such as Coke and Pepsi, in videos. Artists earn money on these product endorsements in their videos. Musicians use these funds to offset the heavy expenses that come with directing and developing a video. Katy's concerns about the products were aimed at how they were placed, conspicuously or nonconspicuously, not about whether or not musicians should use product placements on their work. Katy uses corporate sponsors in her videos regularly and believes adding the products adds to the realism of a photo or video. The comments came after Britney Spears reportedly earned $500,000 in product endorsements from her video for "Hold It Against Me."

Linda Perry, a musician and a songwriter for Pink, Christina Aguilera, and Gwen Stefani, criticized Katy in the press, explaining that "Katy Perry is the worst offender in music today."[14] Despite having several hits off of all her albums, Linda Perry believes that Katy is a one-hit wonder and people only buy singles of her songs and not the whole album. In response, Katy tweeted that there is a lot of interesting words to her songs. Norwegian singer Ida Maria criticized "I Kissed a Girl" when it was released. She said it was not an alluring song and was painful to listen to. Despite her negative remarks, Maria said that she may sing the song as a cover at one of her concerts because the hit did go to number one on the charts.

Rumors also abounded that fellow singer Kelis had bad-mouthed Katy's work. However, Kelis had not spoken in the press in a long time so there was no foundation for the remarks that appeared in a tabloid magazine. Todd Rundgren, a composer, musician, and performer who has worked with such bands as Grand Funk Railroad, Meat Loaf, Badfinger, and the New York Dolls, recently talked about the 2000s pop musicians in an article with *Spinner* magazine. He criticized popular musicians like Katy whose records always seem to have more than one producer behind them. Rundgren described the songs he produced back in the 1970s as being more singer-specific, written from actual experiences in the lives of those musicians. Popular artists, like Rihanna and Katy, are producing songs to their fan bases specifications.

Rundgren stated, "There's no really deep personal messages anymore in a lot of popular music. More than anything they are trying to out-do each other. What is the outrage that will get people buzzing and tweeting?"

Although Katy does not like to be criticized by her fellow musicians, she does take a stand when she feels as if a situation is unfair. She stated her opinion about Kanye West "dissing" Taylor Swift at the MTV Music Awards in 2009. West jumped on stage when Swift was receiving her award for Best Female Video. He told the audience that Beyoncé had the best video of all time. Katy tweeted her fans while she was at the show, saying that she felt bad for Swift and that West was very harsh. When Katy was a guest judge on *American Idol* and fellow judge Kara DioGuardi poked fun at Katy's song "I Kissed a Girl," the two seemed very catty on the show. When DioGuardi started singing Katy's hit "I Kissed a Girl," Katy threatened to throw a Coke on her if she didn't stop. DioGuardi was singing different lyrics to the song than the actual lyrics. The two judges were also very disagreeable on the show, often times not selecting the same contestants to move on.

On the flipside, Katy has also been known to praise fellow musicians in the press. She has used Snoop Dogg and Kanye West in her videos and to produce her songs. Fellow musician Ke$ha was in Katy's "I Kissed a Girl" video. Katy proclaimed in many media outlets that Rihanna is her best friend. After the alleged incident between Rihanna and her then-boyfriend Chris Brown, where Brown allegedly beat Rihanna, the tabloids reported that Katy and Rihanna were always together. Katy commented on the rumors, saying that it is important to have good girlfriends and someone to talk to when things become rough. Katy has said that she will always help her friends in any way that she is needed. Aside from being friends, Katy and Rihanna have also collaborated in the studio. Rumors abounded that the two were teaming up for Rihanna's *Loud* album that was released on November 10, 2010. Rihanna expelled the rumors on a talk show, saying that they had been working on some songs. Rihanna also expressed an interest in going on tour with Katy. She admired all the energy Katy exudes in her performances, which pumps up her fans. "She's a rock star. She has candy and fruit and a blown-up ChapStick onstage, but then she's rocking out with a guitar and banging her head and swinging onstage and crowd-surfing. That's the (stuff) that just makes you excited when you see her perform. She's beautiful, but then she rocks out."[15] In an interview with *Glamour* magazine, Rihanna explained that women were dominating the music charts today, citing the success of herself, Katy, Lady Gaga, and Ke$ha. Rihanna was complimentary of Katy, saying that she enjoyed the way that Katy is honest about everything and always says exactly what she feels.

In 2009, the pair was seen during Paris Fashion Week at two fashion shows, the Jean Paul Gaultier Show and also the Karl Lagerfeld show. Katy valued her time with Rihanna and believes it is important to have down-to-earth friends that can just hang out together.

With any celebrity, rumors are constantly being spread. Allegedly, there was a feud between best friends Rihanna and Katy. Rihanna had made a comment in the press about current music lyrics being generic for most pop stars in the music industry today. The media reported that she specifically cited Lady Gaga, Ke$ha, and Katy Perry. The rumors were fuelled even more when Rihanna was unable to attend the wedding of Katy and Brand. Rihanna tried to clear up the rumors in an interview with *Fabulous* magazine. She claimed she was speaking about the songwriters and producers who write the songs. They pander their lyrics to different singers until someone buys the song. Artists buy songs that suit their creativity. Katy, Rihanna, Ke$ha, and Lady Gaga are eccentric in their different ways and they all have a distinctive sound.

The band Minus the Bear has also publicly touted Katy's talents. They admitted that they listen to Katy's "Teenage Dream" song in their van while they are touring. The band has been looking for a cover song and has been listening to other songs like Metallica's as well, but they genuinely like the lyrics and catchy tune of "Teenage Dream." Keith Urban and actress Nicole Kidman have also been touted as big fans of Katy. The couple believes that Katy's songs are addictive and catchy. Urban went so far as to sing a Katy song at one of his concerts. He and his opening band, The Band Perry, performed "Teenage Dream" at a concert in Regina, Canada.

When Katy was voted number one on *Maxim*'s 2010 Hot 100 list, her credibility with fans, both men and women, went through the roof. She enjoyed all the press that went with the accolade; however, she acknowledges that other quirky musicians could also fit the bill. Lady

Gaga and Ke$ha have a fun-loving quirky style that is sexy and sells music.

Katy vocalized her opinion when she saw some musicians interspersing religion and sexuality in their lyrics. Although she doesn't practice a particular religion, Katy tweeted, "Spirituality and sexuality are two separate things, and then when you decide to put them into the same subject, it gets interesting for people."[16] Katy expressed her thoughts after Lady Gaga's video for "Alejandro" was released. It was misconstrued that Katy was speaking about Lady Gaga's video specifically, when in reality she was speaking generally of musicians, lyrics, and religion. She also commented that she was a big fan of Lady Gaga and realized that everyone has different viewpoints.

Katy helped singer Rebecca Black in the early days of her career. Black appears in Katy's "Last Friday Night (T.G.I.F.)" video. When bloggers were criticizing Black and talking derogatorily about her single "Friday," Katy came to the rescue. She believes Black is destined to be a pop star and advised Black to stay grounded and never forget where she came from, an adage that Katy herself uses to keep things real and down-to-earth. When Miley Cyrus was pictured in the press as allegedly going down a destructive path, media outlets reported that Katy called Cyrus "a Britney Spears." Katy used her Twitter outlet to let the world and her fans know that she never said anything negative about Cyrus and she liked and admired the teenage singer.

Katy realizes her name is an important part of her identity and wants to make it as recognizable as possible. For this reason, in 2004 she changed her name from Katy Hudson to Katy Perry, using her mother's maiden name. She did not want to be confused with blonde actress Kate Hudson. However, there is a Katie Perry in Sydney, Australia, who is a fashion designer. Perry's company was started two years before singer Katy Perry came along. Katy was trying to secure her trademark in Australia, so a routine letter was sent to the fashion designer. "When she (Katy Perry) became famous, Katy's lawyers asked the designer to withdraw her trademark. The designer refused, and the matter hasn't been taken any further."[17] Shortly after the incident with the fashion designer, Katy was interviewed on the Australian TV show *Sunrise*. Katy's manager turned off the power to the stage lights during the interview because she was afraid of the questions Katy may be asked

Katy and Miley Cyrus pose on the red carpet at the MTV Video Music Awards on September 7, 2008. (AP Photo/Chris Pizzello.)

about the trademark incident during the interview. The interview was cut short because of the disruption.

In the spring of 2011, Katy's name was mentioned in an article about a hit-and-run accident in California. Eric Zentner, who appeared in Katy's video for the single "Hot N Cold," was killed on California's Highway 101. Zentner ran out of gas and had left his car to find help. Police believed he was hit by a light blue Dodge Caravan. One of Katy's actors in her "Teenage Dream" video was arrested on suspicion of misdemeanor battery. Josh Kloss portrayed Katy's boyfriend in the video. Kloss was smoking a cigarette outside a shopping mall when he was asked by a security guard to extinguish the cigarette. Unfortunately for Katy, her name always appears in the press when someone she is associated with happens to get their name in the media, whether the topic is negative or positive.

In 2005, a picture was taken of Katy in which she was holding a knife to her cheek. When the picture surfaced on the Internet, campaigners against knife violence in the United Kingdom thought the photos were in bad taste. The photo in questions was taken by acclaimed fashion photographer Terry Richardson and was part of a series of photos that were taken for the cover of Katy's album. The photo came out only a day after 16-year-old Joseph Lappin was fatally stabbed outside a Liverpool youth club. Katy's publicist released a statement that the picture was actually taken in 2005 and had nothing to do with the happenings in Liverpool. Katy took another picture with a spoon on her cheek that she said was to promote eating ice cream. The group also found this photo offensive as well because they felt Katy was making light of a bad situation.

During Katy's *California Dreams* tour, she had Calvin Harris performing as a DJ for some of her shows. However, he withdrew his partnership with the Katy team because of where he was told to perform. Harris was told he would have to DJ on the side of the grand stage for approximately 30 minutes. Because of Twitter, everyone knew of Harris' departure from the tour. When Harris withdrew from the *California Dreams* tour, the two artists took to defending themselves about the whole situation on Twitter. Harris was slated to join the tour for concerts in both Ireland and Britain. His last-minute withdrawal was what sent the artists verbally attacking each other. Harris claimed he was upset that Katy's production team had moved his performance location. In his Tweet comments, he replied to fans saying that Katy's concert was awesome and people will be delighted with the results even if he did not perform at the venues. Shortly after the incident Harris was criticized by Katy's fans for not performing at the concerts. He then made a public apology to Katy and her fans via his Twitter account. He also commented that technology can be a dark thing sometimes, when everyone was bashing him about his decision not to perform.

Katy has had other musicians perform in the same location, such as Marina and the Diamonds, New Young Pony Club, and Yelle, and none of them had a problem with where they had to be. Harris canceled out of all the remaining shows that he was scheduled to perform with Katy. Singer Robyn was also an opening act on the *California Dreams* tour and admires and respects Katy. "For me bigger's not always better, I want to do things where I feel like my integrity of what I do onstage is not compromised, and I knew she was a fan and she wanted me to go on and just do my thing, and that's why I did it. It was an easy decision. If I get to do my thing, there's no place I won't do it. It's great to be on that stage and her audience is amazing," Robyn said about agreeing to be Katy's opening act.[18]

With the advent of new social media, such as Facebook and Twitter, celebrities can take to the computer or mobile phone to express their distaste over something as simple as a comment made in the press. Both Katy and her best friend Rihanna tweeted about a comment made by Kenneth Tong about anorexia. He posted, "To be skinny is perfect and to be fat is unacceptable." In answer to his posts, both musicians commented about girls dying because of anorexia nervosa and people making comments that the world needs to be skinny. Tong argued that he only made the post to get attention and to prove to the marketing world that Twitter is a very powerful marketing tool. Despite his reasons, Tong also angered groups and organizations that deal with health issues such as weight. In an effort to redeem himself, Tong has said he would make a donation to Beat, a "leading UK charity for people with eating disorders and their families."[19]

In her "California Gurls" video, the production crew uses two life-size Gummi Bears. Two Gummi Bears greet Katy with rude, offending gestures. Manufacturing companies of Gummi Bears, Trolli and Haribo, have stated that these are poor imitations and Gummi Bears would never react in such a way if they were made by Trolli or Haribo. Katy, however, likes to be creative in her videos and steps into unchartered territory with her gimmicks to add shock value for her fans. In the video, Katy donned a bra that shot out whipped cream. This was her only defense against Snoop Dogg and his band of evil Gummi Bears. Katy had fun making her outrageous costumes but explained that they did get heavy at times.

Since her marriage to funnyman Brand, Katy has been in the spotlight because of her lyrics, her costumes, and now because of Brand's antics. Brand went to go see Katy for one of her concerts in Japan. He was deported because of incidents that occurred 10 years previously. Both Brand and Katy tweeted about the incident with Katy being upset that Brand was unable to see her show since she had flown him all the way to Japan. She also wanted her followers on Twitter to follow her lead and post "free Rusty Rockets." Despite Brand being deported from Japan, Katy proceeded with her concert. She did not want to disappoint any of her Japanese fans.

Over the New Year holiday in 2011, Brand posted a picture of Katy on Twitter while she was in bed without any make-up. The media had gotten the picture and had called it a not-so-flattering picture of the pop star. Katy immediately had the Twitter picture taken down but not before the public saw it.

Because she is a celebrity, Katy is always being photographed and hounded for statements by magazines and newspapers. A few weeks before she was to wed Russell Brand on September 14, 2010, Katy was at the Los Angeles Airport with Brand. Photographer Marcello Volpe was trying to get a picture of the singer. Brand pushed Volpe, believing that he was trying to take pictures up Katy's skirt. Volpe placed Brand under citizen's arrest until the airport security arrived. Brand was arrested for suspicion of battery and was released after $20,000 in bond was posted. After going to court and meeting with his own lawyers, city prosecutors decided not to press charges against Brand. The incident between the photographer and Brand was caught on tape.

Despite Katy's overwhelming success, she has had her fair share of obstacles down the road. She overcomes the scrutiny and controversy by holding onto her individuality and speaking her mind.

NOTES

1. Jo Berry, *Katy Perry California Gurl* (London: Orion Publishing Group, 2011), p. 47–48.

2. Tim Nixon, "Katy Perry Is Offensive," *The Sun*, June 19, 2009. www.thesun.co.uk.

3. Staff, "Katy Perry: Beth Ditto Is 'Tacky' for Saying I'm Offensive to Gay Culture," *Pink News*, June 4, 2009. www.pinknews.co.uk.

4. "The Men and Women Who Made 2008 a Year to Remember." *Out Magazine*. www.out.com.

5. Internet Movie Database. www.imdb.com.

6. Jocelyn Vena, "Katy Perry Opens Up about Her Background in Grammy Special," *MTV News*, February 3, 2009, www.mtvnews.com.

7. Roger Price, "Katy Perry's Parents Condemn Her Lifestyle While Cashing in on Her Eternal Damnation," *New York Post*, June 11, 2011. www.nypost.com.

8. "Katy Perry Not Liked by Gay Community," *Starpulse*, September 23, 2008, www.starpulse.com.

9. Naimah Jabali-Nash, "Beach Boys Threaten Katy Perry Over 'California Gurls'? No Lawsuit Just Yet." *CBS News*, August 6, 2010, www.cbsnews.com.

10. "Katy's Boobs Traumatize Mom," *The New York Post*, March 28, 2011. www.nypost.com.

11. Jo Berry, *Katy Perry California Gurl*, p. 48.

12. Rya Backer, "Lily Allen Puts Katy Perry Feud to Bed," *MTV News*, January 19, 2009. www.mtv.com/news/articles.

13. Ibid. www.mtvnews.com.

14. Marianne Garvey, "Rocker Linda Perry Disses Katy Perry: 'She's Just Giving Microwave Popcorn,'" *Entertainment Online*, August 22, 2011. www.eonline.com.

15. Jocelyn Vena, "Rihanna Confirms Collabo with Katy Perry, Just Not on *Loud*," *MTV News*, November 2, 2010. www.mtvnews.com.

16. Jocelyn Vena, "Katy Perry Explains her Lady Gaga Blasphemy Tweet," *MTV News*, January 14, 2010. www.mtvnews.com.

17. David Stone, *Russell Brand and Katy Perry: The Love Story*, p. 73.

18. James C. Montgomery, "Katy Perry Tour Was 'An Easy Decision,' Robyn Says." *MTV News*, June 14, 2011. www.mtvnews.com.

19. Greg McKenzie, "Rihanna and Katy Perry Anger at Twitter Anorexia Hoax," *BBC Newsbeat*, January 12, 2011. www.bbc.co.uk.

Chapter 9

BEYOND THE MUSIC

Since the very beginning of her music career, Katy Perry's goal in developing her music and her style is maintaining her individuality. She uses her music and style of dress to gain the attention of her fans and the press to sell her albums.

Even amid the controversial lyrics and scanty dresses, Katy Perry is a successful musician, songwriter, actress, daughter, and wife. Despite her celebrity, she would be the first to tell the world that she is just a normal human being. In an interview with *Entertainment Weekly*, she said, "I definitely am human, I'm flawed. I mean, I've got zits galore! But my main focus? It's music, period. And I'm just getting started."[1]

She has her favorites like everyone else. Her favorite movie is *The Notebook*. She enjoys club sandwiches. She works out at the gym regularly with her personal fitness trainer Harley Pasternak. When she is at home she enjoys watching movies and relaxes by cleaning her house. Katy considers herself a germophobe and is preoccupied with her personal hygiene. Katy is particular about what she eats and also exercises five times a week. Her trainer, Harley Pasternak, has made sure she eats healthy and exercises regularly to keep her frame toned. Katy jumps rope for stamina and does so before concerts. While growing up,

Katy's celebrity crush was *Home Improvement* star Jonathan Taylor Thomas.

Katy is in awe occasionally as to the level of success she has achieved. She is flattered when being compared to actress Zooey Deschanel in the looks department. However, Deschanel was flattered at first when being compared to Katy, but like everything else, it does have its limits. Fans come up to her and mention a bar that they thought they saw her in when reality it was Katy they were looking for. "I think we lead very different lives. At some point I feel like this will stop being a thing. I like the way my life goes. It's sort of strange to be associated with someone that's doing such different stuff than me," Deschanel stated.[2]

Katy was on the cover of the *Cosmopolitan Australia* magazine. She wore a red crop top with a skinny black skirt. Her hair was the traditional black. In the interview with the magazine she talked extensively about her personality and how she acts while she is on tour. She also revealed that she takes a pink blanket with her on tour so she does not get homesick. When she flies, Katy sometimes takes one of her and Russell's cats with her in first class. The animal does get put in a kennel under the seat.

Katy was emulated as a doll in 2008. The doll was designed by fashion designer Jason Wu. Wu and Katy worked together to make the dolls as life-like to Katy as possible. The finished product was a 12-inch-tall Katy, who was dressed in a gold mini-dress, much like the one Katy wore in her "I Kissed a Girl" video. Katy joined other music stars like Britney Spears, Christina Aguilera, and the Spice Girls, who have been turned into play dolls. Katy made *People* magazine's list of Worst and Best Dressed Celebrities of 2009. Both she and Lady Gaga received an accolade for the year's best fashion rebels.

Katy was featured on the cover of the October 2011 issue of *InStyle* magazine. For the spread she had dyed her hair pink. The dress she wore on the cover of the magazine was designed by Emanuel Ungaro, with a Louis Vuitton belt. During the interview, Katy had opened up about who she is, her personality, and her marriage to Brand.

Katy was voted by the public in NME's Greatest Pop Act ever poll. She was ranked among other pop singers such as Madonna, Lady Gaga, Britney Spears, Cyndi Lauper, and Cher. She was also voted number eight on the AskMen's Web site on their "Most Desirable

Women of 2011 List." She is humbled when other musicians comment positively on her work. "Like, the other day I saw on the Internet that Stevie Nicks liked my song E.T. And I was like, Stevie Nicks even knows who I am? I had chills."[3]

In September 2011, Katy was named as an Adidas woman. The company chose women that have taken their dreams to a higher level and let nothing stand in the way of their goals. The women came from all walks of life, including the sports, music, and fashion industries. Katy shared the distinction with tennis star Caroline Wozniacki, DJ Baby G, and Chinese celebrity La Bing Bing.

Katy appeared on the *Forbes* list, "Best Paid Celebrities Under 30," in 2011. She made it in the Top 10 with an estimated $44 million in earnings for the year. Fellow musician Lady Gaga was named number one, worth an estimated $90 million. Katy shares the accolade with Justin Bieber, Beyoncé, and Rihanna, who were also ranked in the Top 10 on the list.

Katy still considers herself a Christian and is grateful for her strict, religious upbringing. When she was 18 years old she had a picture of Jesus tattooed on her wrist. She said of her Jesus tattoo, "It's always going to be a part of me. When I'm playing, it's staring right back at me, saying 'Remember where you came from'."[4] She learned the lesson early that in order to be successful she had to work hard and focus and especially be willing to sacrifice. Despite giving her career her all, she makes time for other things like getting married and spending holidays with her family. She also enjoys making mixed CDs for her friends.

On November 12, 2010, Katy launched a new perfume called Purr. The perfume debuted in London. Katy was on hand for the unveiling and signed perfume boxes for the first 100 customers. Katy sees the perfume as another way to express her individuality. "Purr is a natural in my style, my tastes and my love for all things incredibly cute. It is an absolutely purrfect perfume that I hope leaves you meowing with delight."[5]

She also entertains her fans by participating in the trends of the moment. In 2011, Katy took part in a ritual called planking. The game has people posting pictures of themselves lying still like a plank of wood. Katy posted a picture of herself on Twitter, planking on the top of a boat. She had donned a bikini top and shorts. Planking was a part of Katy and Brand's Fourth of July celebration in 2011.

Katy compared herself to an artichoke in one of the magazine articles she was interviewed for. She stated that there is so much more to her than what people see. Katy doesn't care what the press says about her, either positively or negatively. Katy has gauged her success by what music critics have said about her work, by the sold-out concerts she performs, and by the number of record sales and downloads.

Katy views herself as a successful musician. She has acted on television and in movies. There has been talk about Katy doing a fashion line as an extension of all the things that she is doing now. Katy nixed this idea for the moment because she is doing so many other things to promote herself. "If I were to juggle another ball, I might end up losing all the balls. I don't feel like there's a ticking time bomb on my career. I don't have to get everything done yesterday."[6]

Katy has just scratched the surface of her success with two platinum albums. She continues to entertain her fans with concerts while having fun, even on the topic of death—she has expressed a desire to have her ashes put into a firework and shot over the Santa Barbara coast in recognition of her song "Firework." She has left an impression and been a firework and inspiration to many teenagers. Her enthusiasm and zest for life was only enhanced by the early setbacks in her career. "My motto from then on after Nashville was to live life to the fullest, because at the end you're dead."[7]

NOTES

1. Leah Greenblatt, " 'Girl' On Top," *Entertainment Weekly*, August 1, 2008, p. 29.

2. James Montgomery, "Zooey Deschanel Wants You to Know That She's Not Katy Perry," *MTV News*, April 2, 2009. www.mtvnews.com.

3. Michael Steele and Editors, *All About Katy Perry, Us Weekly Special Edition*, September 2011, p. 44.

4. Internet Movie Database. www.imdb.com.

5. Jo Berry, *Katy Perry California Gurl* (London: Orion Publishing Group, 2011), p. 234.

6. Todd Plitt, "A Long Kitty Purry Article," *USA Today*, June 6, 2011. www.usatoday.com.

7. David Stone, *Russell Brand and Katy Perry: The Love Story*, (London: John Blake Publishing, 2010), p. 74.

APPENDICES

DISCOGRAPHY

Katy Hudson (released October 23, 2001, by Red Hill Records)

1. "Trust in Me"
2. "Piercing"
3. "Search Me"
4. "Last Call"
5. "Growing Pains"
6. "My Own Monster"
7. "Spit"
8. "Faith Won't Fail"
9. "Naturally"
10. "When There's Nothing Left"

One of the Boys (released June 17, 2008, by Capitol Records)

1. "One of the Boys"

2. "I Kissed a Girl"

3. "Waking Up in Vegas"

4. "Thinking of You"

5. "Mannequin"

6. "Ur So Gay"

7. "Hot N Cold"

8. "If You Can Afford Me"

9. "Lost"

10. "Self Inflicted"

11. "I'm Still Breathing"

12. "Fingerprints"

Teenage Dream (released August 24, 2010, by Capitol Records)

1. "Teenage Dream"

2. "Last Friday Night (T.G.I.F.)"

3. "California Gurls" (with Snoop Dogg)

4. "Firework"

5. "Peacock"

6. "Circle the Drain"

7. "The One that Got Away"

8. "E.T."

9. "Who Am I Living For?"

10. "Pearl"

11. "Hummingbird Heartbeat"

12. "Not Like the Movies"

Katy Perry: MTV Unplugged (released November 17, 2009, by Capitol Records)

1. "I Kissed a Girl"

2. "Ur So Gay"

3. "Hackensack"

4. "Thinking of You"

5. "Lost"

6. "Waking Up in Vegas"

7. "Brick by Brick"

FILMOGRAPHY

Television

The Young and the Restless (2008). In episode 8914, Katy plays herself. Katy does a photo shoot at the magazine *Restless Style*. She is supposed to be the feature story and appear on the cover of the magazine, but there is some indecision whether investors would like a pop star on the cover.

Wildfire (March 12, 2008). Katy plays herself in Season 4, episode 8, "Life's Too Short." An ABC Family show about horse farms, romance, and drama. Katy plays guitar and sings in the club at the beginning of the episode before the opening credits.

American Idol. Katy has been both a performer and a guest judge on this popular talent show. On May 13, 2009, Katy sang "Waking Up in Vegas," in a cape that read "Adam Lambert" on the back. On April 21, 2011, Katy went back to the *American Idol* stage to perform "E.T." She was a guest judge during the auditions in Los Angeles and also filled in and judged the show in August 2009 and in January 2010.

The X Factor. Katy performed "Firework" on the British talent show on October 18, 2010. In 2010, Katy was also a guest judge on the show, sitting beside Simon Cowell, Cheryl Cole, and Louis Walsh. She was sitting in for judge Dannii Minogue while she was on maternity leave. In May 2011, Dannii Minogue decided that she would no longer be a judge on *The X Factor* because it interferes with her obligations with the television show *Australia's Got Talent.* Judge Louis Walsh had said that he would like to see Katy Perry and Sharon Osbourne become permanent judges on the show.

Sesame Street (2010). Katy performs a song with Elmo like other celebrities before her have done. The duo sings a song about opposites to the tune of Katy's song "Hot N Cold." Katy is dressed in a white gown that is low cut. The episode was never aired because of parental concerns that Katy's dress is too revealing for a preschool show. The snippet had been seen by viewers on YouTube who then complained that it was not appropriate for *Sesame Street*.

Saturday Night Live (September 27, 2010). Katy guest-starred on the season opener of *Saturday Night Live*. She performed two of her songs live, "California Gurls" and "Teenage Dream." She also appeared in a parody skit made to poke fun at her *Sesame Street* debacle. She wore a shirt in the skit with Elmo on the front and the neckline torn to her cleavage.

The Simpsons (2010). In the episode titled "The Fight Before Christmas," Katy plays herself and plays the girlfriend of Moe, the bartender. Wearing a red dress with a picture of the Simpsons family on it, Katy appears as her real-life self in the Simpsons house. She kisses Mr. Burns, to which he replies, "I kissed a girl and I liked it." She and Moe are supposed to be housesitting while the Simpsons go to Hawaii for Christmas. At the end of the show the cast sings "The 39 Days of Christmas." Playing on Katy's *Sesame Street* fiasco, they dedicate the show to a special letter and number, as *Sesame Street* does in every episode.

How I Met Your Mother (2011). Katy plays Honey, Zoey's good-looking, flaky cousin. By batting her eyes, she easily gains the affection of Barney, who tries to woo her by telling her he has four Nobel prizes.

Many of Katy's songs have been used in television shows and films. Below is a list of songs, what programs they have been on, and in what year they were used.

"Teenage Dream"

Four episodes of *The Tonight Show* with *Jay Leno*		2011
90210	Episode "Liars"	2011
Glee	Episode "Never Been Kissed"	2010
Saturday Night Live		2010
ES.TV HD		2010
So You Think You Can Dance Canada	Top 14 Performance	2010
The Album Chart Show	"Katy Perry: T4 Special"	2010
Late Show with David Letterman		2010

"I Kissed a Girl"

Saturday Night Live		2008

The Album Chart Show	"Katy Perry: T4 Special"	2010
The X Factor		2010
EastEnders		2010
Live from Studio 5		2010
Glee	"Pilot"	2009
The Inbetweeners	"Work Experience"	2009
20 to 1	"Adults Only 20 to 01: Saucy Songs"	2009
Dancing with the Stars	"Round 2"	2008
So You Think You Can Dance	"Results Show"	2008

"Firework"

The Tonight Show With Jay Leno		2011
Glee	"Silly Love Songs"	2011

"Hot N Cold"

Dancing Stars		2011
90210	"Hollywood Forever"	2008
So You Think You Can Dance	"Top 10"	2008
The Proposal		2009
Ghost Whisperer	"Slow Burn"	2009
Live from Studio 5		2010
Copycats		2010
Alvin and the Chipmunks: The Squeakquel		2009
American Pie Presents: The Book of Love		2009
The Ugly Truth		2009
America's Got Talent	"Audition Show #1"	2009

"E.T."

90210	"It's High Time"	2011

"Waking Up in Vegas"

90210	"One Party Can Ruin Your Whole Summer"	2009
The Amazing Race	"Amazing Grace. How Sweet the Sound."	2009
Greek	"The Wish Pretzel"	2009
Alan Carr: Chatty Man		2009

"If You Can Afford Me"

90210	"Lucky Strike"	2008
When in Rome		2010

"California Gurls"

Glee	"The Sue Sylvester Special"	2011
From Prada to Nada		2011
Saturday Night Live		2011
Saturday Night Live		2010
The Amazing Race	"Hi. I'm sorry. I'm in a Race."	2010
So You Think You Can Dance Canada	"Top 20 Perform"	2010
The Album Chart Show	"Katy Perry: T4 Special"	2010
Late Show with David Letterman		2010

"Peacock"

The Album Chart Show	"Katy Perry: T4 Special"	2010

"Fingerprints"

Baby Mama		2008

"Use Your Love"

The Vampire Diaries	"Under Control"	2010
Endless Bummer		2009

"Thinking of You"

The Vampire Diaries	"Pilot"	2009
Live from Studio 5		2010

"If We Ever Meet Again"

Melrose Place	"Sepulveda"	2010

"Starstrukk"

Live from Studio 5		2010
When in Rome		2010

Film

The Smurfs (released July 29, 2011). Although *The Smurfs* television show was banned in the Hudson household while Katy was growing up because of its evil and sorcery, Katy jumped at the chance to play the voice of Smurfette in the Columbia Pictures film. The film is about the evil Gargamel chasing the Smurfs out of their village. The group lands into real-life Central Park so they have real-life adventures while trying to get back to their village before Gargamel finds them. The real-life characters are played by Neil Patrick Harris and Jayma Mays. Other voice-over actors include Jonathan Winters as Papa Smurf; George Lopez as Grouchy Smurf; Kevin James as Hefty Smurf; Alan Cumming as Gutsy Smurf; and Hank Azaria as Gargamel.

The Muppets (released November 23, 2011). Katy makes an appearance in this new Muppet movie. The film stars Jason Segel and Amy Adams. Tex Richman plans to drill for oil underneath the Muppet theater. Because the Muppets have broken up, three people try to get the Muppets back together and save the theater. Katy is not the only celebrity that makes a cameo appearance. Liza Minnelli and Whoopi Goldberg also make appearances in the movie.

AWARDS AND NOMINATIONS

2011	APRA Music Award	Nominated for International Work of the Year for "California Gurls" with Snoop Dogg
2011	ASCAP Pop Music Award	Won Most Performed Song for "Teenage Dream"
2011	ASCAP Pop Music Award	Won Most Performed Song for "California Gurls" with Snoop Dogg
2011	People's Choice Award	Won for Favorite Online Sensation
2011	Billboard Music Award	Nominated for Fan Favorite Award
2011	Billboard Music Award	Won for Top Hot 100 Artist
2011	Billboard Music Award	Won for Top Digital Songs Artist
2011	Billboard Music Award	Nominated for Top Radio Songs Artist
2011	Billboard Music Award	Nominated for Top Female Artist
2011	Billboard Music Award	Nominated for Top Pop Artist
2011	Billboard Music Award	Nominated for Top Hot 100 Song for "California Gurls" with Snoop Dogg
2011	Billboard Music Award	Nominated for Top Digital Song for "California Gurls" with Snoop Dogg

2011	Billboard Music Award	Nominated for Top Pop Song for "California Gurls" with Snoop Dogg
2011	Billboard Music Award	Nominated for Top Pop Song for "Firework"
2011	Billboard Music Award	Nominated for Top Pop Song for "Teenage Dream"
2011	Billboard Music Award	Won for Top Pop Album for *Teenage Dream*
2011	Brit Award	Nominated for International Female Artist
2011	Brit Award	Nominated for International Album for *Teenage Dream*
2011	Glamour Women of the Year	Won for Best Solo Artist Award
2011	Grammy Award	Nominated for Album of the Year for *Teenage Dream*
2011	Grammy Award	Nominated for Best Pop Vocal Album for *Teenage Dream*
2011	Grammy Award	Nominated for Best Female Pop Vocal Performance for "Teenage Dream"
2011	Grammy Award	Nominated for Best Pop Collaboration with Vocals for "California Gurls" with Snoop Dogg
2011	International Dance Music Award	Nominated for Best Solo Artist
2011	International Dance Music Award	Nominated for Best Music Video for "Firework"
2011	International Dance Music Award	Nominated for Best Pop Dance Track for "Firework"
2011	Juno Award	Won International Album of the Year for *Teenage Dream*
2011	MTV Video Music Award	Won for Video of the Year for "Firework"
2011	MTV Video Music Award	Won for Best Collaboration for "E.T." with Kanye West

2011	MTV Video Music Award	Nominated for Best Female Video for "Firework"
2011	MTV Video Music Award	Nominated for Best Pop Video for "Last Friday Night (T.G.I.F.)"
2011	MTV Video Music Award	Won for Best Special Effects for "E.T." with Kanye West
2011	MTV Video Music Award	Nominated for Best Direction in a Video for "E.T." with Kanye West
2011	MTV Video Music Award	Nominated for Best Art Direction in a Video for "E.T." with Kanye West
2011	MTV Video Music Award	Nominated for Best Editing in a Video for "E.T." with Kanye West
2011	MTV Video Music Award	Nominated for Best Cinematography in a video for "Teenage Dream"
2011	MTV Video Music Award	Nominated for Best Video with a Message for "Firework"
2011	MuchMusic Video Award	Nominated for International Video of the Year for "E.T."
2011	MuchMusic Video Award	Nominated for Most Watched Video of the Year for "California Gurls" with Snoop Dogg
2011	MuchMusic Video Award	Nominated for Most Watched Video of the Year for "Teenage Dream"
2011	Nickelodeon Kids' Choice Award	Won Favorite Female Singer
2011	Nickelodeon Kids' Choice Award	Nominated for Favorite Song for "California Gurls" with Snoop Dogg
2011	People's Choice Award	Won for Favorite Female Artist
2011	People's Choice Award	Nominated for Favorite Pop Artist
2011	People's Choice Award	Won for Favorite Internet Sensation
2011	People's Choice Award	Nominated for Favorite Song for "California Gurls" with Snoop Dogg
2011	People's Choice Award	Nominated for Favorite Music Video for "Teenage Dream"
2011	Soul and Jazz Award	Nominated for Next Hit of 2011 for "E.T."

2011	Soul and Jazz Award	Won for Music Video of the Year for "Teenage Dream"
2011	Soul and Jazz Award	Won for Single of the Year for "Teenage Dream"
2011	Soul and Jazz Award	Nominated for Best Artist of the Year Act Pop
2011	Soul and Jazz Award	Won for Artist of the Year
2011	Soul and Jazz Award	Won for Album of the Year for *Teenage Dream*
2011	Soul and Jazz Award	Nominated for Best Album Pop of the Year for *Teenage Dream*
2011	Teen Choice Award	Won for Choice Music: Female Artist
2011	Teen Choice Award	Nominated for Choice Music: Single for "Firework"
2011	Teen Choice Award	Nominated for Choice Music: Love Song for "Teenage Dream"
2010	ASCAP Pop Music Award	Won for Most Performed Song for "Waking Up in Vegas"
2010	ASCAP Pop Music Award	Won for Most Performed Song for "Hot N Cold"
2010	American Music Award	Nomination for Artist of the Year
2010	American Music Award	Nomination for Favorite Pop/Rock Female Artist
2010	American Music Award	Nomination for Favorite Pop/Rock for *Teenage Dream*
2010	ARIA Music Award	Nominated for Most Popular International Artist
2010	Grammy Award	Nomination for Best Female Pop Vocal Performance for "Hot n Cold"
2010	International Dance Music Award	Nominated for Best Solo Artist
2010	MTV Europe Music Award	Nominated for Best Female Artist
2010	MTV Europe Music Award	Nominated for Best Pop Artist

2010	MTV Europe Music Award	Nominated for Best World Stage Artist
2010	MTV Europe Music Award	Won for Best Video for "California Gurls" with Snoop Dogg
2010	MTV Europe Music Award	Nominated for Best Song for "California Gurls" with Snoop Dogg
2010	MTV Video Music Award	Nominated for Best Female Video for "California Gurls" with Snoop Dogg
2010	MTV Video Music Award	Nominated for Best Pop Video for "California Gurls" with Snoop Dogg
2010	MuchMusic Video Award	Nominated for Best International Artist Video for "Waking Up in Vegas"
2010	MuchMusic Video Award	Nominated for International Video of the Year for "Starstrukk" with 3OH!3
2010	People's Choice Award	Nominated for Favorite Pop Artist
2010	Soul and Jazz Award	Won Hit of the Year for "Teenage Dream"
2010	Soul and Jazz Award	Won for Best Collaboration for "California Gurls" with Snoop Dogg
2010	Soul and Jazz Award	Nominated for Best Artist of the Year Pop Act
2010	Soul and Jazz Award	Nominated for Best Album Pop of the Year for *One of the Boys*
2010	Soul and Jazz Award	Nominated for Album of the Year for *One of the Boys*
2010	Teen Choice Award	Nominated for Choice Summer: Female Artist
2010	Teen Choice Award	Nominated for Choice Fashion: Female Hottie
2010	Teen Choice Award	Nominated for Choice Fashion: Red Carpet Fashion Icon Female
2010	Teen Choice Award	Won for Choice Music: Single for "California Gurls" with Snoop Dogg
2010	Teen Choice Award	Won for Choice Summer Song for "California Gurls" with Snoop Dogg

2010	Teen Choice Award	Nominated for Choice Music: Hook Up for "If We Ever Meet Again" with Timbaland
2009	ASCAP Pop Music Award	Won for Most Performed Song for "I Kissed a Girl"
2009	ASCAP Pop Music Award	Won for Most Performed Song for "Hot N Cold"
2009	Brit Award	Won for International Female Artist
2009	Glamour Women of the	Nominated for Aussie Hair Care Year Award Newcomer of the Year
2009	Grammy Award	Nomination for Best Female Pop Vocal Performance for "I Kissed a Girl"
2009	International Dance Music Award	Nominated for Best Pop Dance Track for "I Kissed a Girl"
2009	International Dance Music Award	Nominated for Best Alternative/Rock Dance Track for "I Kissed a Girl"
2009	MTV Europe Music Award	Nominated for Best Female Artist
2009	MTV Europe Music Award	Nominated for Best Video for "Waking Up in Vegas"
2009	MTV Video Music Award	Nominated for Best Female Video for "Hot n Cold"
2009	MuchMusic Video Award	Nominated for Best International Artist Video for "I Kissed a Girl"
2009	MuchMusic Video Award	Nominated for People's Choice: Favorite International Video for "Hot N Cold"
2009	Nickelodeon Kids' Choice Award	Nominated for Favorite Song for "I Kissed a Girl"
2009	People's Choice Award	Won for Favorite Pop Song for "I Kissed a Girl"
2009	Teen Choice Award	Nominated for Choice Music: Album for *One of the Boys*
2009	Teen Choice Award	Nominated for Choice Music: Single for "Hot N Cold"

2009	Teen Choice Award	Nominated for Choice Music: Female Artist
2008	MTV Europe Music Award	Nominated for Most Addictive Track for "I Kissed a Girl"
2008	MTV Europe Music Award	Won for Best New Act
2008	MTV Video Music Award	Nominated for Best Art Direction for "I Kissed a Girl"
2008	MTV Video Music Award	Nominated for Best Cinematography for "I Kissed a Girl"
2008	MTV Video Music Award	Nominated for Best Editing for "I Kissed a Girl"
2008	MTV Video Music Award	Nominated for Best Female Video for "I Kissed a Girl"
2008	MTV Video Music Award	Nominated for Best New Artist
2008	Teen Choice Award	Nominated for Choice MySpacer
2008	World Music Award	Nominated for World's Best Selling Pop/Rock Female Artist
2008	World Music Award	Nominated for World's Best Selling New Act

INTERPRETATION OF LYRICS

Katy's lyrics have always been a topic of discussion and sometimes controversy. Below is a list of her songs, along with summaries and comments. This provides a comparison of what she did in her early music career to what she does today. However, there are no interpretations for her *Katy Hudson* album as they were all written around her Christian upbringing. Her first album is also hard to find since the record company had declared bankruptcy. A musician's songs are their way of communicating their feelings to the outside world. Katy is no different, as her songs are an extension of her. In interviews with the press she openly talks about wearing her emotions on her sleeve and putting her real-life experiences in her lyrics. However, there are many songs on both of her albums for which Katy has not expressed the true meaning behind them.

One of the Boys (released June 17, 2008, by Capitol Records)

1. "One of the Boys": The title track on the album with the same name, "One of the Boys" is Katy's coming of age track. In her childhood, Katy acted like a tomboy but then transformed in her teenage years. She began experimenting with makeup and clothes and looked for a style that suited her. In the beginning of the song she mentions all the things that she has in common with boys. The middle of the song relates everything that a teenage girl does to make herself look attractive. Finally, at the end of the lyrics, Katy professes that she no longer wants to be one of the boys.

2. "I Kissed a Girl": This song sparked controversy but also made Katy a household name. She was asked several times in interviews if she had kissed a girl. In some interviews she denied that she had and in other interviews she said she had. She admitted to Katie Couric that she kissed a girl. Katy has said she wrote this song about teenage girls and how they can be very touchy-feely and are more intimate in their relationships than men. The song was inspired by both actress Scarlett Johansson and a friendship that Katy had when she was 15 years old. In an interview with *The New Gay* website, Katy explained the background of the song. She commented, "Everyone takes the song and relates it to their situation, they can see it however they want to see it. Love it, hate it, for me it was about us girls. When we're young we're very touchy feely. We have slumber party sing-alongs, we make up dance routines in our pajamas. We're a lot more intimate in a relationship than guys can be. It's not perverse but just sweet, that's what the song is about."[1]

3. "Waking Up in Vegas": Inspired by a life of living on the edge, "Waking Up in Vegas" has a bit of irresponsibility about it. Katy equates this song with going out with your friends or boyfriend one night and getting wild and spontaneous and waking up in another state or town. According to some reports, when she was 21, Katy went to Vegas to pretend to get married and as a prank sent the pictures to her family, friends, and producer. This was the song that told Capitol Records executive Chris Anokute that Katy had a special talent for singing and entertaining.

4. "Thinking of You": Katy wrote this song by herself and it was produced by Butch Walker. It is a song about never knowing who the best person is and always settling for second best. The single is a pop ballad song that includes acoustic instruments. Unfortunately, this was the only one of Katy's singles that did not place in the Top 10 on the music charts. The single also sold less than one million copies in the United States., a record-breaking low for Katy and her music.

5. "Mannequin": This song is about the same man that Katy wrote about in the song "Ur So Gay." Katy has difficulty getting close to the man she is in a relationship with and believes he is just going through the motions. The man she is dating is stoic and seldom shows or relates his true feelings. She performed the song live in 2008 at the KISS FM Sprint Live Lounge.

6. "Ur So Gay": In this controversial hit, Katy sings about a relationship that she was in with a man that had many tendencies that a gay man would have. Katy intended the song to be a joke and believes the world is metrosexual. Many groups and critics were appalled by the lyrics and thought the song made fun of the lesbian and gay lifestyle. Others were offended that Katy was talking about the gay community when she, herself, was not gay and could not possibly know what it means to be a gay man or woman.

7. "Hot N Cold": This song represents the ups and downs of a relationship at any given time. Katy uses her own past relationships in many of her songs. "Hot N Cold" uses opposites to reflect the cliché that opposites attract. There are several versions of this song where some of the harsher words are replaced by toned-down lyrics. Katy performed the first live presentation of this song on the *Today* show. In the video, Katy is left at the altar and then chases her groom all around the town. Eventually, at the end of the video, it is revealed that it was all a dream of the groom's, and the congregation and the bride are still waiting on the altar for his "I do."

8. "If You Can Afford Me": As Katy became more successful, she had a lot more confidence in who she was and the respect she should

In 2008, Katy performs at Rockefeller Plaza in New York on the Today *show. (AP Photo/ Richard Drew, file.)*

be given as a musician and as a woman. The song relates this feeling of getting what she wants and that she is deserving of all that she gets and accomplishes.

9. "Lost": Katy wrote this song when she woke up one morning after a night of partying. Although Katy has never vocalized what the inspiration was behind this song, many have speculated it is about Katy going out and pursuing her dream. She tries to pray but thinks it may be useless, seeing as how she does not profess and follow one particular religion. In her quest to be successful, she only has the friends she parties with and wonders if they would be her friends if she didn't party all the time with them.

10. "Self-Inflicted": This is a song about getting the man in a relationship to pay attention to the woman. Katy has never spoken openly about the meaning behind this song, but critics believe the song is about domestic abuse. The lyrics relate to doing anything, even getting hurt, to win the love of a man. She talks about

scars and bruises throughout the song. She sings about wild antics and adventures that are gone through.

11. "I'm Still Breathing": This song was co-written with Dave Stewart, who was in the band Eurythmics. The song was actually produced and recorded in London, England. "I'm Still Breathing" is one of Katy's more sad and melancholy songs on the *One of the Boys* album. It is about a dead relationship that a couple is still in and the need to get out of the relationship before either one of them gets hurt. The songs "I'm Still Breathing" and "Thinking of You" were written with the same ex-boyfriend in mind. Katy uses a lot of imagery to get her point across on this track.

12. "Fingerprints": Written with Greg Wells, this song is about figuring out one's identity with all the adventures and obstacles along the way. Katy has grown up in the music industry and changed many times along the way. She changed her musical genre, her fashion style, and has even changed her hair color several times in order to find something she is confident with. She also makes these changes to keep her audiences entertained and interested. Although Katy has never talked openly about these lyrics in the press, she has allowed the song to be used as the theme song for the Oxygen television series *Fight Girls*.

Teenage Dream (released August 24, 2010, by Capitol Records)

1. "Teenage Dream": A song about being in love as a teenager, "Teenage Dream" was the second single released from the *Teenage Dream* album. Katy and Bonnie McKee wrote the song with youth in mind and tried to relate to what every teenager is going through. Katy sang the song with her youth and her upcoming wedding to Russell Brand in mind. The combination of the two led to a song that talks about being so in love, it makes someone feel youthful like a teenager. Katy enjoyed writing this song because it made her think of all her own teenage dreams and gave her respite in the midst of a year of putting out an album and planning for her wedding.

2. "Last Friday Night (T.G.I.F.)": Katy was inspired to write this song after she had a night of partying where she could vaguely recall the events from the night before. "There's nothing better

than an impromptu dance party with my friends. My track 'Last Friday Night (T.G.I.F.)' is a song about debauchery because I had one of those nights in Santa Barbara. We went out to this place called Wildcat and got crazy. We had a couple of beers and danced until we died, then brought the party back to the hotel room."[2] Katy included celebrities Kenny G., Corey Feldman, and Debbie Gibson, among others, in the video. Katy's alter ego, Kathy Beth Terry, also appears in the video.

3. "California Gurls": Katy recorded this song with Snoop Dogg. The inspiration for this song was Jay-Z and Alicia Key's song "Empire State of Mind" about New York. Katy felt there needed to be a song about California. It takes into account the beach life-style of the West Coast and the laid-back approach California has to offer. In the song, Snoop Dogg sings, "I wish they all could be California Girls," in a tribute to the women of California. This line also caused controversy with the original singers of the line, The Beach Boys. The odd spelling of "Gurls" is in remembrance of musician Alex Chilton of the band Big Star who died in 2010. Big Star recorded the song "September Gurls" in 1974.

4. "Firework": Katy considers this song her most important hit on the *Teenage Dream* album. It is an inspirational anthem that many organizations have adopted to encourage people to make a difference in the lives of others. Katy was influenced in writing this song by Jack Kerouac's book *On the Road*. Kerouac's novel is about road trips and the adventures or misadventures along the way. During his travels, he enjoyed coming across those that were charismatic and had a "spark" about them. The song has a great message. The line "like a firefly" in the original song was changed to "like the Fourth of July." This has added a patriotic feel to the song that inspires people even more. Katy also sings the line "like the Fourth of July" because it has more emotion and stir with her audience. The single was also played at the Miss American Pageant.

5. "Peacock": Capitol Records did not want this track on the *Teenage Dream* album because of its controversial lyrics. Katy wrote this song with the individuality of a peacock, the bird, in mind. She also wanted to have fun with words when she penned

this song. She saw the song as a gay anthem with the message that being yourself was okay. There are a number of ways to interpret the song. In an interview with *MTV News,* she commented, "With me there a lot of double entendres. There's a lot of puns. You know, when I learned how to write a song, the person that was kind of teaching me was an amazing songwriter and he was like, 'Don't forget about the double entendres. Don't forget about the puns. Don't forget that one word can have two meanings.' So I'm always kind of looking for that one thing that's really normal that you can make twisted."[3] Katy premiered her controversial "Peacock" song in Malaysia on the MTV World Stage in August 2010. The song was added to her *Teenage Dream* album at the last minute. Katy claimed it is the world's biggest innuendo song. She produced the song with the Swedish production team Stargate.

6. "Circle the Drain":The literal story of "Circle the Drain" is a drug addiction that puts a strain on a relationship. Katy never revealed who the song referred to, but many in the media speculated that the hit was about Katy's relationship with band member Travis McCoy of Gym Class Heroes. McCoy has never listened to the song but has heard the rumors that the song may refer to him, to which he said, "At least the song has substance." During Katy and McCoy's one-year, on-again-off-again relationship, Katy had helped the singer with a bout of depression. In the chorus, Katy sings that instead of having a serious relationship, she has to take care of the person like a mother.

7. "The One That Got Away": In the song "The One That Got Away," there are similarities between the lyrics and events that took place in Katy's teenage years. Katy believes that this song is different than her other singles and reflects a different side of her. This song is about promising yourself to someone forever and then not being able to follow through. "The One That Got Away" single was released in the fall of 2011. The cover of the single featured Katy with pink hair and a sophisticated pin-up look. Katy put together the *Teenage Dream* album in a mere six months, so she extracted many of her song ideas and lyrics from her own life experiences.

8. "E.T.": Rapper Kanye West is featured on this song. The beat to the song was discovered accidentally in the studio. Katy had wanted to write a futuristic song and thought that the beat was perfect for what she wanted to accomplish. The background to the song is about falling in love with a foreigner. The song is filled with extraterrestrial metaphors. At one point in the track, Katy sings "Fill me with your poison," which could be interpreted as wanting to be abducted by aliens. West sings two verses of the song. Music critics see this as one of Katy's darker singles, revealing a deeper, more mature artist.

9. "Who Am I Living For?": This ballad was written by Katy, Christopher Stewart, Monte Neuble, and the bass player for the band I Am Ghost, Brian Telestai. Katy never interprets this song on her Web site or in interviews, but there is evidence of her Christian upbringing when she references the Old Testament figure Queen Ester.

10. "Pearl": Written also with Christopher Stewart and Greg Wells, this was the last song written for the *Teenage Dream* album. Katy felt that the song "Pearl" completed her album and it was the one gem missing from the album. She explained to *MTV News*, "I did one more song with Greg Wells, and it was called 'Pearl.' And it was kind of just like, 'All right, now I have this crown, and I have all these jewels, and I can put these little jewels into the crown, and I feel like it's a complete presentation, something I'm really proud of'."[4]

11. "Hummingbird Heartbeat": Katy's songs are inspired by love and her relationships. Brand had an impact on many of the love songs on the *Teenage Dream* album. "Hummingbird Heartbeat" is about how fast the heart flutters when someone is in love and the effect love has on a person's emotions and activities. In real life, hummingbirds have the highest metabolism of any other animal and their heart rate can reach as fast as 1,260 beats per minute. In a *BBC Newsbeat* interview, Katy said, "There are some songs on the album inspired by love. "There's a song called Hummingbird Heartbeat. He gives me that Hummingbird Heartbeat."[5]

12. "Not Like the Movies": Katy finished writing "Not Like the Movies" when she first started dating Russell Brand. The song is

about a relationship where a woman is just going through the motions in life and is still waiting for her knight in shining armor. In the lyrics, Katy is telling her fans that there is someone out there for everyone and a person deserves all the glitter and romance that happens in a good love film. Katy believed she found her celebrity crush in Brand as through their engagement and wedding he was a gentleman and a romantic.

NOTES

1. "The Men and Women Who Made 2008 a Year to Remember," *Out Magazine*. www.out.com.

2. "Katy Perry Says Streaking Inspired Album Track," *MTV News-United Kingdom*, March 10, 2011. www.mtv.co.uk.

3. Jocelyn Vena with Sway Calloway, "Katy Perry Says 'Peacock' Is 'The World's Biggest Innuendo'," *MTV News*, August 24, 2010. www.mtvnews.com.

4. Jocelyn Vena, "Katy Perry Says 'Pearl' Is Her Album's Crowning Jewel," *MTV News*, August 23, 2010. www.mtvnews.com.

5. Greg Cochrane with interview with Natalie Jamieson, "Katy Perry's Album 'Inspired' by Partner Russell Brand," *BBC Newsbeat*, July 15, 2010. www.bbc.co.uk.

BIBLIOGRAPHY

BOOKS ABOUT KATY PERRY

Berry, Jo. *Katy Perry California Gurl*. London: Orion Publishing Group, 2011, 236.

Brown, Anne. *Katy Perry*. People in the News Series. New York: Lucent Books, 2011, 112.

Steele, Michael and Editors. *All About Katy Perry. Us Weekly Special Edition*. September 2011, 78.

Stone, David. *Russell Brand and Katy Perry: The Love Story*. London: John Blake Publishing, 2010, 325.

ARTICLES ABOUT KATY PERRY

Apodaca, Rose. "What Katy Perry Did Next." *Harper's Bazaar*, December 2010, 86–291.

Greenblatt, Leah. " 'Girl' On Top." *Entertainment Weekly*, August 1, 2008, 27–29.

Grigoriadis, Vanessa. "Sex, God and Katy Perry." *Rolling Stone Magazine*, August 19, 2010, 40–47.

Hedegaard, Erik. "Little Miss Sunshine." *Rolling Stone Magazine*, July 2011, 68–74.

Hedegaard, Erik. "Sexy Beast." *Rolling Stone Magazine*, June 10, 2010, 58–63, 88–89.

Hilton, Ruth. "Number One Crush." *Maxim*, January 2011, 54–59.

Long, April. "Fantastic Voyage." *Elle*, March 2011, 399–403, 484.

Prato, Alison. "Katy Perry: Head Over Heels." *Cosmopolitan*, November 2010, 35–38.

Robinson, Lisa. "Katy Perry's Grand Tour." *Vanity Fair*, June 2011, 160–168, 209.

Tozzi, Carissa Rosenberg. "Katy Perry." *Seventeen Magazine*, September 2010, 190–195.

INTERNET

Adler, Shawn. "Katy Perry, P. Diddy among Celebrities to Unite in Support of Red Cross as Japan Reels." *MTV News*, March 13, 2011. www.mtvnews.com.

Allison, Vicky. "Katy Perry Struggles to Stay Vegetarian." *Monsters and Critics*, August 22, 2011. www.monstersandcritics.com.

AllMusic.com Website www.allmusic.com.

Atkinson, Claire. "Katy Perry Takes Crown as No. 1 'Dream' Queen." *New York Post*, August 18, 2011. www.nypost.com.

Backer, Rya. "Lily Allen Puts Katy Perry Feud to Bed." *MTV News*, January 19, 2009. www.mtv.com/news/articles.

Beale, Lauren. "Katy Perry, Russell Brand Find Buyer for Los Feliz Home." *Los Angeles Times*, July 27, 2011. www.latimes.com.

Bhansali, Akshay. "Katy Perry Calls Kaskade's 'Teenage Dream' Remix 'Fantastic'." *MTV News*, September 17, 2010. www.mtvnews.com.

Bhansali, Akshay. "Katy Perry Is Jealous of Taylor Swift's Part in VMA Promo." *MTV News*, August 17, 2009. www.mtvnews.com.

Blanco, Alvin. "Katy Perry, Kayne West Share Best Collaboration VMA." *MTV News*, August 28, 2011. www.mtvnews.com.

Boone, John and Casablanca, Ted. "Rebecca Black Gets Advice from Katy Perry & Won't Fight Back against Bloggers with Her Music." *Entertainment Online*, August 30, 2011. www.eonline.com.

"Calvin Harris Pulls out of DJ Slot on Katy Perry Tour." *BBC Newsbeat*, March 29, 2011. www.bbc.co.uk.

Charlesworth, Jenny. "Minus the Bear Confesses Their Love for Katy Perry, Consider Doing Metallica Cover." *AOL News*, September 19, 2011. www.aolnews.com/tag/katy-perry/.

"China Bans Lady Gaga, Katy Perry and Backstreet Boys Hits." *The Huffington Post*, August 25, 2001. www.huffingtonpost.com.

Cochrane, Greg, with interview with Natalie Jamieson. "Katy Perry's album 'Inspired' by Partner Russell Brand." *BBC Newsbeat*, July 15, 2010. www.bbc.co.uk.

Della Cava, Marco R. "Katy Perry Is One Hit Away from a Broken Record." *USA Today*, August 18, 2011.www.usatoday.com.

Dinh, James. "Katy Perry's Geeky Teen Alter Ego Joins Twitter, Facebook." *MTV News*, June 7, 2011. www.mtvnews.com.

Dinh, James. "Katy Perry's 'Part of Me' Leaks Online." *MTV News*, December 30, 2010. www.mtvnews.com.

Drury, Sharareh. "Katy Perry Goes Home with a 'Grammy' No Matter What." *Entertainment Online*, February 13, 2011. www.eonline.com.

Dumitrescu, Andrei. "Just Dance 3 Sponsors Katy Perry's California Dreams United Kingdom Tour." September 13, 2011. www.onenewspage.com.

Eger, Andrea. "Katy Perry Offers Sweet, Satisfying Performance." *Tulsa World*, September 19, 2011. www.tulsaworld.com.

Epting, Chris. "Todd Rundgren Dismisses Pop Acts Like Katy Perry, Rihanna Focus on Innuendos, Not Messages." *AOL News*, September 15, 2011. www.aolnews.com.

Fowler, Brandi. "Charges Filed over Katy Perry and Russell Brand's Raucous Wedding." *Entertainment Online*, October 30, 2010. www.eonline.com.

Fowler, Brandi. "Katy Perry and Russell Brand: The Weirdest Wedding Gift Ever?!" *Entertainment Online*, October 30, 2010. www.eonline.com.

Ganz, Caryn. "Katy Perry Goes Full Urkel on 'Last Friday Night' Cover." *The Amplifier*, May 3, 2011. new.ca.music.yahoo.com.

Garvey, Marianne. "Rocker Linda Perry Disses Katy Perry: 'She's Just Giving Microwave Popcorn'." *Entertainment Online*, August 22, 2011. www.eonline.com.

Gibson, Cristina. "Katy Perry's 'Firework' Video Not Just about Sparkly Boobs." *Entertainment Online*, October, 28, 2010. www.eonline .com.

Gibson, Cristina. "Russell Brand Reveals Why Marriage to Katy Perry Works." *Entertainment Online*, December 5, 2010. www.eonline .com.

Garibaldi, Christina with Jocelyn Vena. "Selena Gomez 'Had to Fight' to Get Katy Perry Song 'Rock God'." *MTV News*, September 22, 2010. www.mtvnews.com.

Gray, Mark. "Katy Perry Celebrates Bachelorette Party in Vegas." *People*, September 19, 2010. www.people.com.

Greene, Andy. "Katy Reveals Plans for California Dreams World Tour." *Rolling Stone*, January 27, 2011. www.rollingstone.com.

Grossberg, Josh and English, Whitney. "Versace Model Featured in Katy Perry Video Dead in Hit and Run." *Entertainment Online*, April 1, 2011. www.eonline.com.

Haberman, Lia. "See Katy Perry as a 13-Year-Old Nerd." *Entertainment Online*, June 8, 2011. www.eonline.com.

Hodgson, Grant. "Katy Perry Loves Her 'Pink Blanket'." *MTV News*, September 5, 2011. www.mtvnews.com.

Internet Movie Database www.imdb.com

Izundu, Chi Chi. "Louis Walsh Wants Katy Perry as New Judge on X Factor." *BBC Newsbeat*, May 15, 2011. www.bbc.co.uk.

Jabali-Nash, Naimah. "Beach Boys Threaten Katy Perry Over 'California Gurls'? No Lawsuit Just Yet." *CBS News*, August 6, 2010. www.cbsnews.com.

Jenison, David. "Hot 100 Seals Its 1,000 Hit with Katy's 'Kiss'." *Entertainment Online*, June 26, 2008. www.eonline.com.

"Jewel and Friends Donate Song Lyrics to Charity Auction." *Look to the Stars*, December 5, 2008. www.looktothestars.org.

Joy, Kevin. "Katy Perry: Pop Diva Delivers with Sweetness, Spice." *The Columbus Dispatch*, September 14, 2011. www.dispatch.com.

"Katy Perry and Friends Design T-shirts for AIDS," *Look to the Stars*, May 8, 2009. www.looktothestars.org.

"Katy Perry and Friends Perform on Adoption Special." *Look to the Stars*, December 20, 2010. www.looktothe stars.org.

"Katy Perry and Justin Bieber to Rock Jingle Ball for Charity." *Look to the Stars*, November 23, 2010. www.looktothestars.org.

"Katy Perry and Paramore to Headline USO Celebrity Charity Concert." *Look to the Stars*, November 16, 2010. www.looktothestars.org.

"Katy Perry and Pink Donate Shoes for Landmine Charity." *The Daily Mail*, July 18, 2010. www.dailymail.co.uk.

"Katy Perry and Russell Brand Want to Start a Charity." *Teen Music*, December 25, 2010. www.teenmusic.com.

"Katy Perry Breaks US Billboard Chart Record." *BBC Newsbeat*, May 17, 2011. www.bbc.co.uk.

"Katy Perry Falls Ill, Cancels Chicago Show; Concedes Diva Showdown to Britney." *The Huffington Post*, July 8, 2011. www.huffingtonpost.com.

"Katy Perry Goes Pink for Breast Cancer Awareness." *Look to the Stars*, October 8, 2010. www.looktothestars.org.

"Katy Perry Is the Real Deal." *Fabulous Magazine*, December 2008. www.fabulousmag.co.uk.

"Katy Perry Not Liked by Gay Community." *Starpulse*, September 23, 2008. www.starpulse.com.

"Katy Perry Performs While Stars Shoot Hoops for Charity," *Look to the Stars*, February 16, 2009. www.looktothestars.org.

"Katy Perry Says Streaking Inspired Album Track," *MTV News-United Kingdom*, March 10, 2011. www.mtv.co.uk.

"Katy Perry Signs Guitar for Charity." *Look to the Stars*, May 25, 2009. www.looktothestars.org.

"Katy Perry Will be WonderWoman?" December 20, 2010. www.katy-perry.us/2010/12/.

"Katy Perry's Teen Choice Awards Outfits." *BBC Newsbeat*, August 9, 2010. www.bbc.co.uk.

"Katy Turns Charity Efforts to Flood Victims." www.charity-charities.org.

"Katy's Boobs Traumatize Mom." *The New York Post*, March 28, 2011. www.nypost.com.

Katy's Official Website www.katyperry.com.

Kaufman, Amy. "Russell Brand: A New Brand." *Los Angeles Times*, April 7, 2011. www.latimes.com.

Kaufman, Gil. "Katy Perry, Avril Lavigne Sit in on Tame *American Idol* LA Auditions." *MTV News*, January 26, 2010. www.mtvnews.com.

Kaufman, Gil. "Katy Perry's *Sesame Street* Skit Canned." *MTV News*, September 23, 2010. www.mtvnews.com.

Kaufman, Gil. "*Songs for Japan* Raises $5 Million for Earthquake Relief." *MTV News*, May 4, 2011. www.mtvnews.com.

Kaufman, Gil. "VMA Nominee Leader Katy Perry, by the Numbers." *MTV News*, July 22, 2011. www.mtvnews.com.

"Lady Gaga Wears a Red Meat Bikini." *Rising Stars*, September 7, 2010. www.risingstarstv.net.

Malkin, Marc. "Glee: Darren Criss and Katy Perry 'Dream' Together." *Entertainment Online*, December 6, 2010. www.eonline.com.

"The Men and Women Who Made 2008 a Year to Remember." *Out Magazine*. www.out.com.

McKenzie, Greg. "Rihanna and Katy Perry Anger at Twitter Anorexia Hoax." *BBC Newsbeat*, January 12, 2011. www.bbc.co.uk.

McKinley, James C. "China Says Lady Gaga, Beyoncé and Other Pop Stars Are a Threat." *The New York Times*, August 26, 2011. www.nytimes.com.

McKinley, James C. "Katy Perry Makes Some Billboard History." *The New York Times*, August 17, 2011.www.nytimes.com.

Montgomery, James C. "Katy Perry Denies Calling Lady Gaga 'Calculated'." *MTV News*, August 24, 2009. www.mtvnews.com.

Montgomery, James C. "Katy Perry Dishes on Her 'Long and Winding Road' from Singing Gospel to Kissing Girls." *MTV News*, June 24, 2008. www.mtvnews.com.

Montgomery, James C. "Katy Perry Explains Her Link to Kelly Clarkson's New Album." *MTV News*, April 16, 2009. www.mtvnews.com.

Montgomery, James C. "Katy Perry Opens Up about her Friendship with Rihanna." *MTV News*, April 10, 2009. www.mtvnews.com.

Montgomery, James C. "Katy Perry Talks about her Split from Travis McCoy . . . Sort Of." *MTV News*, January 9, 2009. www.mtvnews.com.

Montgomery, James C. "Katy Perry Talks Wedding 'Myths' at EMA 2010." *MTV News*, November 7, 2010. www.mtvnews.com.

Montgomery, James C. "Katy Perry Tour Was 'An Easy Decision,' Robyn Says." *MTV News*, June 14, 2011. www.mtvnews.com.

Montgomery, James C. "Travie McCoy Finally Addresses Katy Perry's 'Circle the Drain'." *MTV News*, October 1, 2010. www.mtvnews .com.

Montgomery, James C. "Zooey Deschanel Wants You to Know That She's Not Katy Perry." *MTV News*, April 2, 2009. www.mtvnews .com.

Montgomery, James C. with Akshay Bhansali. "Ryan Tedder Writing 'Roller-Rink Skating Party' Songs for Katy Perry." *MTV News*, April 9, 2010. www.mtvnews.com.

Mulick, Marcus. "Katy Perry's Intestinal Woes Shut Down Shows." *Entertainment Online*, July 8, 2011. www.eonline.com.

Mullins, Jenna. "Russell Brand Deported from Japan." *Entertainment Online*, May 22, 2011. www.eonline.com.

Ngo, Ella. "Katy Perry Accessorizes Her Lips with Holiday Bling." *Entertainment Online*, December 3, 2010. www.eonline.com.

Ngo, Ella. "Katy Perry on Russell Brand: I Found Me a 'Great Man of God'." *Entertainment Online*, November 3, 2010. www.eonline .com.

"Quick Takes: Katy Perry Makes History." *Los Angeles Times*, August 18, 2011. www.latimes.com.

Plitt, Todd. "A Long Kitty Purry Article." *USA Today*, June 6, 2011. www.usatoday.com.

Price, Richard. "Katy Perry's Parents Condemn Her Lifestyle While Cashing in on Her Eternal Damnation." *New York Post*, June 11, 2011. www.nypost.com.

Reid, Jefferson. "Katy Perry Twitpic Posted by Hubby, Hastily Yanked Down." *Entertainment Online*, January 2, 2011. www.eonline .com.

Reid, Shaheem. "Timbaland Tells Story Behind Katy Perry Duet, 'If We Ever Meet Again', " *MTV News*, December 10, 2009. www .mtvnews.com.

Rodriguez, Jayson. "Katy Perry Reveals 'Darker Side' in Racy Photo Spread." *MTV News*, May 28, 2009. www.mtvnews.com.

Rosen, Zack. "Music: Katy Perry: *The New Gay* Interview." *The New Gay*, June 10, 2008. www.thenewgay.net.

Rothstein, Simon. "Katy Perry is a F***ing Thieving Slut," *The Sun*, August 4, 2009. www.thesun.co.uk.

"Russell Brand Launches Company Branded Films." *The Huffington Post*, August 9, 2011. www.huffingtonpost.com.

Saunders, Tim. "Grammy Charity Auction Set to Rock." *Look to the Stars*, February 5, 2009. www.looktothestars.org.

Saunders, Tim. "Stars Attend Life Ball for AIDS in Austria." *Look to the Stars*, May 18, 2009. www.looktothestars.org.

Saunders, Tim. "Stars Want to be Millionaires for Charity." *Look to the Stars*, August 3, 2009. www.looktothestars.org.

Scudder, Annie. "The Origins of Smurfette." *The Huffington Post*, July 26, 2011. www.huffingtonpost.com.

Serpe, Gina. "Katy Perry-Russell Brand Cheating Claim—Katy (and the Truth) Poke Holes in Report." *Entertainment Online*, April 28, 2011. www.eonline.com.

Serpe, Gina. "More Is More. Katy Perry Shows off Lavender Locks and Four Different Looks at the VMAs. *Entertainment Online*, August 29, 2011. www.eonline.com.

Serpe, Gina. "Russell Brand and Katy Perry Headed to Splitsville?! Couple Hit Back at 'Trash' Tabloids." *Entertainment Online*, July 18, 2011. www.eonline.com.

Serpe, Gina. "So True? So False? Five Wackiest Rumors about the Katy Perry-Russell Brand Wedding." *Entertainment Online*, October 26, 2010. www.eonline.com.

Sinkevics, John. "Katy Perry Takes Ill; Refunds Available for Tonight's Grand Rapids Show at Van Andel Arena." *The Grand Rapids Press*, September 11, 2011. www.mlive.com.

"Smurfs Sequel Already in the Works after Success of Cartoon Movie, Starring Katy Perry, Hank Azaria, George Lopez, Jonathan Winters." *The Huffington Post*, August 10, 2011. www.huffingtonpost.com.

"Stars Sign Hardhats for Charity Auction." *Look to the Stars*, February 24, 2009. www.looktothestars.org.

Stewart, Ella. "Bitch Stole My Look: Katy Perry vs. Dita Von Teese." *Entertainment Online*, May 9, 2011. www.eonline.com.

Stewart, Scott. "Katy Perry Gets Sugarcoated by All the Gimmicks at AllState Arena." *Chicago Sun-Times*, August 20, 2011. www.suntimes.com.

Trust, Gary. "Eminem, Rihanna Top Hot 100 for Fifth Week." *Billboard Magazine*, August 19, 2010. www.billboard.com.

Tschorn, Adam. "Can You be Too Sexy for Certain Situations?" *Los Angeles Times*, October 3, 2010. www.latimes.com.

Turner, Sadao. "Russell Brand: Katy Perry's 'Atrocious' Acting Led to Her Being Cut from Greek." Ryan Seacrest Online, June 4, 2010. www.ryanseacrest.com.

Vena, Jocelyn. "*American Idol* Guest Judge Katy Perry 'Didn't Make Anybody Cry'." *MTV News*, September 23, 2009. www.mtvnews.com.

Vena, Jocelyn. "DJ AM 'Left a Really Wonderful Legacy,' Katy Perry Says." *MTV News*, August 31, 2009. www.mtvnews.com.

Vena, Jocelyn. "How Katy Perry Avoided a Sophomore Slump." *MTV News*, December 30, 2010. www.mtvnews.com.

Vena, Jocelyn. "Katy Perry Brings Candyfornia to *Today*." *MTV News*, August 27, 2010. www.mtvnews.com.

Vena, Jocelyn. "Katy Perry Explains Her Lady Gaga Blasphemy Tweet." *MTV News*, January 14, 2010. www.mtvnews.com.

Vena, Jocelyn. "Katy Perry Featured in New Will Cotton Exhibit." *MTV News*, January 14, 2011. www.mtvnews.com.

Vena, Jocelyn. "Katy Perry Follows Lady Gaga in Mermaid Trend." *MTV News*, July 12, 2011. www.mtvnews.com.

Vena, Jocelyn. "Katy Perry Isn't Dating Josh Groban." *MTV News*, March 25, 2009. www.mtvnews.com.

Vena, Jocelyn. "Katy Perry 'May Take Over the World,' *The Smurfs* Co-Stars Say." *MTV News*, July 26, 2011. www.mtvnews.com.

Vena, Jocelyn. "Katy Perry Opens Up about Her Background in Grammy Special," *MTV News*, February 3, 2009. www.mtvnews.com.

Vena, Jocelyn. "Katy Perry, Pink, Hayley Williams Bash Kanye West's VMA Rant." *MTV News*, September 14, 2009. www.mtvnews.com.

Vena, Jocelyn. "Katy Perry Poses in Lingerie, Talks Religion in *Rolling Stone*." *MTV News*, August 3, 2010. www.mtvnews.com.

Vena, Jocelyn. "Katy Perry Praises Lady Gaga, Ke$ha in *Maxim*." *MTV News*, December 9, 2010. www.mtvnews.com.

Vena, Jocelyn. "Katy Perry Reveals Tour Will Have 'Smell-o-Vision'." *MTV News*, January 27, 2011.www.mtvnews.com.

Vena, Jocelyn. "Katy Perry, Russell Brand Laugh Off Pregnancy Rumors." *MTV News*, January 31, 2010. www.mtvnews.com.

Vena, Jocelyn. "Katy Perry Says 'Pearl' Is Her Album's Crowning Jewel." *MTV News*, August 23, 2010. www.mtvnews.com.

Vena, Jocelyn. "Katy Perry Says She's Taking Russell Brand's Name." *MTV News*, December 8, 2010. www.mtvnews.com.

Vena, Jocelyn. "Katy Perry Says She's Tamed 'Professional Prostitute Russell Brand," *MTV News*, July 6, 2010. www.mtvnews.com.

Vena, Jocelyn. "Katy Perry Sees 'All Kinds of Emotions' in Her Fans." *MTV News*, April 6, 2011. www.mtvnews.com.

Vena, Jocelyn. "Katy Perry Serenades Models at Victoria Secret Fashion Show." *MTV News*, November 11, 2010. www.mtvnews.com.

Vena, Jocelyn. "Katy Perry 'So Excited' about Nine VMA Nods." *MTV News*, July 21, 2011. www.mtvnews.com.

Vena, Jocelyn. "Katy Perry Takes a Vow of Celibacy." *MTV News*, January 21, 2009. www.mtvnews.com.

Vena, Jocelyn. "Katy Perry's 'Last Friday Night' Invite Thrills Hanson." *MTV News*, June 14, 2011. www.mtvnews.com.

Vena, Jocelyn. "Rihanna and Katy Perry Vacation Together in Barbados." *MTV News*, April 22, 2009. www.mtvnews.com.

Vena, Jocelyn. "Rihanna Confirms Collabo with Katy Perry, Just Not on *Loud*," *MTV News*, November 2, 2010. www.mtvnews.com.

Vena, Jocelyn. "Russell Brand Says Katy Perry's MTV Movie Awards Song Is 'Brilliant'." *MTV News*, January 3, 2010. www.mtvnews.com.

Vena, Jocelyn. "Weezer's River Cuomo Working with Katy Perry." *MTV News*, October 15, 2009. www.mtvnews.com.

Vena, Jocelyn with Sway Calloway. "Katy Perry Says 'Peacock' Is 'The World's Biggest Innuendo'." *MTV News*, August 24, 2010. www.mtvnews.com.

Warner, Kara and Jem Aswald. "Katy Perry's 'California Gurls' Gummi Bears Are Rude, Crude Imitations, Haribo Says," *MTV News*, June 17, 2010. www.mtvnews.com.

Warner, Kara and Sway Calloway. "Katy Perry Recalls Grueling Makeup Process for 'E.T.' Video," *MTV News*, March 31, 2011. www.mtvnews.com.

Ziegbe, Mawuse. "Katy Perry Shares Russell Brand Wedding Footage at the Grammys." *MTV News*, February 13, 2011. www.mtvnews.com.

INDEX

About the Author

KIMBERLY DILLON SUMMERS is a freelance writer and editor and full-time mother residing in Rockford, IL. She graduated from Iowa State University with a degree in Journalism and Mass Communication. She is a former editor of NTC/Contemporary Publishing, where she worked on the popular *Chase's Calendar of Events*. She has written *Miley Cyrus: A Biography*, published in 2009, and *Justin Timberlake: A Biography*, published in 2010, for the Greenwood Press Biography Series. She wrote *United Kingdom* for ABDO Publishing Country Series. She has written biographical information for the Internet site allmusic.com. Her articles have also been published by The Bridges Initiatives, Inc., and she creates newsletters and writes financial articles for Rock Valley Federal Credit Union located in Loves Park, IL.